Download the audiobook for free!

I really appreciate you downloading my book, and since you took action I am going to give you my audiobook version 100% FREE!

To download, visit:
http://www.self-publishingpro.com/blf-audiobook

SELF-PUBLISHING PRO

NOW IT'S YOUR TURN

Discover the EXACT 3-step blueprint you need to become a bestselling author in 90 days.

No matter if you stink at writing, have zero free time, or have no clue where to begin, you CAN become a best-selling author and build the life of your dreams.

With success across a variety of different niches and professions, Self-Publishing Pro is the only tool you will need to come out to finish your book and be victorious!

Make sure to watch this FREE VIDEO TRAINING SERIES now, and you too can become a best selling author

Self-PublishingPro.com/FreeTraining

Giving Is Our Duty

10% of author royalties are donated between 3 nonprofit charities:

FrontRowFactor.com is a charity that creates incredible once-in-a-lifetime experiences for kids and adults with life-threatening illnesses by giving them a Front Row experience at the live event of their dreams.

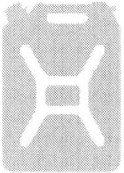

charity: water

CharityWater.org, where 100% percent of the donations go to providing clean water to people in need.

Coral.org, a 4 Star Charity that works hard to protect our most valuable and threatened ecosystem, coral reefs.

BOOK LAUNCH FORMULA: How to Write, Publish, & Market Your First Non-Fiction Book (Around Your Full Time Schedule)

Justin Ledford

Copyright 2017 by Justin Ledford. All Rights Reserved.

No part of this publication may be reproduced or transmitted in any form or by any means, mechanical or electronic, including photocopying and recording, or by any information storage and retrieval system, without permission in writing from the author or publisher (except by a reviewer, who may quote brief passages and/or show brief video clips in a review).

Disclaimer: The advice and strategies contained herein may not be suitable for every situation. This work is sold with the understanding that the Author and Publisher are not engaged in rendering legal, accounting, or other professional services. Neither the Author or the Publisher shall be liable for damages arising herefrom, The fact that an organization or website is referred to in this work as a citation or a potential source of further information does not mean that the Author or the Publisher endorses the information that the organization or website may provide or recommendations it may make. Further, readers should be aware that Internet websites listed in this work may have changed or disappeared between when this work was written and when it is read.

Interior Design: Matt Duncan, MattDuncan.co

ISBN-10:0-9975050-2-8

ISBN-13:978-0-9975050-2-3

Endorsements

"A VERY PRACTICAL AND EASY TO IMPLEMENT GUIDE ESPECIALLY FOR SOON TO BE AUTHORS!

This book is will act a simple roadmap that you can follow to get your first book done. I highly recommend experienced authors and first-time authors read this and follow along."

-- Hal Elrod, #1 Best Selling author of ***The Miracle Morning***

"WRITE YOUR BOOK!

Everyone has their own unique story to tell. Sometimes you just don't know when, where and how to start. The best time to start is always NOW - you'll find the HOW in Justin's simple approach on how to get your book done fast!"

-Marc Reklau #1 Best Selling Author of ***30 Days - Change your habits, Change your life***

"HE MAKES A TOUGH TOPIC EASY TO UNDERSTAND

Justin's approach makes writing, marketing and publishing your first book into an easy to understand process. No matter what level of skill you have, Justin's laid back teaching approach will help you finish your book fast."

-Matt Duncan, Author of ***The Upcycled Toys Club***

"Inspiring read!

Really well done. If you trust in the process and you'll see yourself finishing your book by using Justin's approach. Would recommend this book to anyone to help them get unstuck."

-Jenna Bayne, Author of ***I Am Part of Nature***

"Book Launch Formula was filled with incredibly insightful information.

These techniques helped me stay laser focused when I wrote my book. It will show you exactly what you need to know to get your book done. Prepare to be impressed!"

-Brianna Greenspan, Best Selling Author of *The Miracle Morning: Art of Affirmations*

"Great resource to move forward!!!!!

This book gave me direction in creating an action plan! Using the strategies I was able to finish my book fast. I highly recommend this book!

-Natalie Janji, #1 Amazon Best-Selling Author of *The Miracle Morning for College Students*

"I highly recommend Book Launch Formula!

It is incredibly helpful because it gives you a detailed step by step process to both write and market your own book. Buy and read it immediately!"

John Ruhlin, Best Selling Author of *Giftology*, Founder of Ruhlin Group

Table of Contents

Endorsements	x
Table of Contents	1
Introduction	2
Chapter 1: The Type of Money You Can Make	7
Chapter 2: If Others Can Do It So Can You	14
Chapter 3: Conquering Misguided Beliefs	19
Chapter 4: How I Came to Write My First Book	24
Chapter 5: Why Timing Is Perfect	28
Chapter 6: The Different Reasons People Write Books	33
Chapter 7: 4 Ways of Creating a Book Idea	43
Chapter 8: Refining Your Book Idea	50
Chapter 9: Creating a Bestselling Book Title and Subtitle in 7 Easy Steps	57
Chapter 10: Brainstorm to Outline	67
Chapter 11: Writing a Sales Driven Introduction	75
Chapter 12: Start Writing & Finish Your Rough Draft ASAP	79
Chapter 13: The Different Stages of Editing	87
Chapter 14: Format Your Book and Prepare for the Big Day	99
Chapter 15: Designing a Cover That Will Sell Your Book	103
Chapter 16: Generating Excitement About Your Book	108
Chapter 17: Launching Your Book The Pro Way	112
Chapter 18: Tips On How To Become A Best Selling Author	119
Chapter 19: Writing a Book Will Transform Your Life	125
Chapter 20: Market Your Book Like A Business	130
Chapter 21: It's Time To Get In The Game!	136
Acknowledgments	139

Introduction

I want to congratulate you for taking time to learn how to self-publish your book. Whatever reason you have for mastering the skill of self-publishing I want to let you know that in this book you will learn everything you need to know to ensure that your book will be a good and a successful one. All you have to do is follow the steps and recommendations outlined here.

You will learn exactly how to write, publish, and market your book all while working around a full-time job.

If I can become a #1 best-selling author on Amazon with a demanding work schedule, and family I love spending time with, so can you.

I will teach you a concise step-by-step approach for writing your book despite a busy schedule. Whatever you're calling in life is you will benefit from the strategies and techniques which have allowed me and countless others to generate the kind of success most only dream of - just by learning to effectively write books on a part time basis.

Brianna, a successful salesperson from Texas says, "The techniques taught in this book are exactly what helped me to finish my first book in less than 3 months and become an Amazon #1 best-seller - earning residual income month after month."

I learned a lot from my first two books, and am now working on my third - using the steps that got the greatest results. I promise that if you act on the steps outlined in the following pages you will not only finish your book faster than you imagined possible, you will enjoy the process.

I can also promise that the results you achieve will allow you to live a more fulfilling life, helping you become an authority in your current profession, and boosting your income.

Don't be the kind of person who has dreams of writing a book, but never sees them through. Instead, be someone who crosses writing their book off their bucket list, and then moves on to even bigger and greater achievements.

If I can write and launch my second book as an inexperienced writer with a crazy schedule - so can you.

You should read this book if:
- You believe you have a story to tell
- You have a full-time job/profession and don't feel you have any extra time to write.
- Writing a book is on your wish list
- You have a business and want to be identified as the "go-to expert" in your field
- You have no idea where to get started, but have a desire to write your book
- You want to follow a proven path for successfully publishing your first book
- You want to build a passive income on a part-time basis
- You have already published a book and want to know how to market it

Let's go ahead and talk about who this book is not for.

This book is not for you if:
- You want to publish your book without using Amazon (I recommend this as essential to your success, and I will explain why in detail later in this book)
- You want this to be a get-rich-quick scheme (it is worthwhile, but it does take work)
- You're not willing to commit 30 minutes to an hour a day for 90 days (you can take days off, but when you do work on your book you must be committed to apply 30 minutes of focused effort)

With that out of the way, if you still feel you're in the right place - keep reading.

Have You Ever Considered Launching Your Own Book?

If your answer is "yes", then you are in the perfect place, at the right time, and you should really do it now because writing a book has never been easier.

We all have a story inside of us, and the reason you want to publish a book is because you have one to tell. I want to help you bring that story to the masses.

By the time you finish reading this book you will understand the book launch formula which will help you complete your book and make it a success. I learned the industry tricks which make up this formula from mentors who are some of the best in the industry, as well as from personal experience. Most of us started just like you, without an idea of what to write or how to publish it, but with a willingness to learn.

Every morning when I work out I listen to authorities in the self-publishing industry like Hal Elrod, Tim Ferriss, Steve Scott, Honoree Corder, James Altucher, Pat Flynn, and many more.

I have tested their ideas and witnessed firsthand what works and what doesn't work.

Reading this book will save you so much time because I have done all the research for you. I will be providing you with the best strategies from the many books, seminars, and instructional videos which I used to learn about self-publishing.

I will be straightforward with you and tell you only what strategies work best and what you should spend your time doing. These approaches are tried and true - they have been tested and proved to work for me and many others.

It's okay if you feel like you don't know where to begin - I am going to teach you everything that you need to know, and walk you through the process from beginning to end.

Why I Wrote This Book

Do you realize how much information exists on the Internet dealing with the subject of writing books?

There are over 32 books on "how to write an outline", and a mind-boggling 40,000 plus articles on "how to overcome writer's block".

If you are busy like me you probably don't have time to weed through all this material – and you won't have to! I put together **Book Launch Formula** to provide you with a simple, easy to follow plan.

I have met people who started writing a book but never finished because they got stuck, and didn't know how to push through the different stages of the writing process.

The good news is that if you follow the steps exactly as I lay them out for you, it will be easy for you to complete your book.

I will make sure that you don't fall victim to misinformation and hyper-inflated claims about how much money people are making by self-publishing their books.

Some people claim that you can write a book in as little as 7 days and make $15,000 a month from Kindle books, and yes, it *is* possible and there are people doing it.

But the real story is that those people are either well known authors or on-line celebrities who have published dozens of books and have a large following already.

My intention is to help the brand new, first-time author who wants to do this part-time just like I did. Right now, the only difference between those full-time authors and you is they got started a little earlier.

Here's the deal. I live by the belief that everything new is a little bit challenging until it becomes easy. And publishing a book is no different. The good news is that I am going to break the process down into simple steps for you to follow.

CHAPTER 1

The Type of Money You Can Make

Shortly after my first book launched, I was free diving in Cabo San Lucas with some of my friends. One of them heard about my successful book launch, and asked with great interest, Justin, can you actually make money writing a book?

I could confidently answer, while we were diving and chilling on the beach yesterday, I made over $50.

It was only as those words left my mouth that I truly realized what was happening. My book was generating a steady passive income mailbox money that just shows up every month!

People are still curious and call me regularly to see if my book is still making money after the launch, once the momentum faded away.

I believe it's important that I bring this up because there is a lot of misinformation about passive income.

My friends and family ask me how much money they can make if they write a book and my answer is always the same.

It's impossible to give you an exact amount so much depends on how passionate you are about it, what you're interested in, and the category you choose to write for.

Some people are making as little as a $2 a day while other are making as much as $2,500 each day.

My first book **Visions to The Top** is about using visualization and meditation to achieve heightened levels of success in business and in life. It falls into a very specific niche - targeting people who believe in miracles, the law of attraction, or those interested in how people like Michael Phelps, Arnold Schwarzenegger, and top CEO's use visualization techniques.

I wanted to bring this up so that you can be aware that this is not a massive audience.

If my book fell into a niche with a much larger audience - like health and fitness, relationships, time management, stress management, or money-making strategies - then the chances of me making more money is extremely high because there are more potential readers for books on these subjects.

You may personally not want to write about any of these subjects either, and that's OK. I didn't, and I am still managing to generate a steady, passive income.

So how much money am I really making? And why is passive income so important?

Before we dive into the successful formula for exactly how to write and publish a book, I want to spend a little time talking about passive income and the importance of having it in your life.

Having a monthly check deposited in your bank account every month can provide you with both personal and financial freedom. There is nothing more satisfying than doing a job once and getting paid for it month after month for years to come.

You never know who is going to share your book on their social media. Look what happened to Eckhart Tolle when he wrote "A New Earth: Awakening to Your Life's Purpose". Once Oprah read it and said it was great he became an overnight success, and his financial life changed forever.

To this day, he continues to make money from a book he wrote years ago!

Before I go ahead and teach you the **Book Launch Formula** in the next section, I want to illustrate what passive income would mean for you.

Let's imagine, for example, that you have $48,000 in your bank account. In today's market, banks are typically offering an interest rate of only .01% annually. This means that after keeping your $48,000 in the bank for an entire year, you would have only earned $480 in passive income.

Now, here is the real interesting part. You can write a book that generates you a measly $200 a month, which would translate to you earning $2400 a year. You would have to keep $240,000 in a bank account for a full year to get the same amount of return.

What sounds easier? Taking 90 days to write a book in your spare time and making $200+ a month in passive income, or finding $240,000 to put in a bank account and keep it there?

Once I realized the power of passive income, the decision to write books was a no brainer. Reflect for a minute on my results:

I wrote my book in 90 days and it generates around $487.76 every month (and much more when I market it) in passive income. Here's the math $487.76 x 12 months = $5853.12 in profit each year. I'd have to keep $585,000 in my bank account earning .01% interest, to do as well!

Don't you think that writing a book around your spare time sounds a lot easier than coming up with $500k? Of course you do! My passionate belief that it is essential to create a source of passive income is inspired by a family member who has worked for the city for over 25 years. She is planning to retire when she hits 30 years, at which time the company will give her a pension which amounts to $1200 a month.

Thirty years of hard work for $1200 a month! If someone follows the approach I teach in the following chapters and writes 6 books in let's just say 3 years (that's just 2 books a year) they could earn the same income or more passively, as my family member who has worked hard for 30 years.

You should also know that I have my book in several formats, and I can help you figure out if this is a good option for you or not. It has been published as an e-book, a paperback and audiobook.

I sell from 1 to 9 copies each day starting at $0.99 going upwards to $2.99. When it's priced from $0.99 - $1.99 I make a 35% royalty, when it's priced at $2.99 I make a 70% royalty.

Later on in the book, I'll explain why it's important to change the price of your book every so often.

After looking at all the spreadsheets and doing the math I'm making over $400 a month from my first book, with an average of $295.44 per month from Kindle alone.

This same book is making an average of $117.69 as an audiobook, and $74.63 as a paperback.

This amounts to $487.76 on average per month, and yes, that's not a "quit your job" sum - but consider that I launched my book with no audience, that it was my first try, and that I did it very part time.

The analytic research I did early on told me to expect $300-$400 dollars month from my niche, so I'm glad to say I surpassed the expected amount. All of this will become clearer as we go along, and once you complete the exercise outlined in chapter 7 which will show you how to come up with different book ideas you'll will realize that if passive income is your main objective, you will want to write multiple books.

What else could you do with a limited investment of time and money, and have it generate several thousands of dollars a year extra for you? There are not many investments out there that can give you the type of return a book can, without a high risk.

Take real estate, for example. I have several friends who average 9-10% on their rental returns as real estate investors, but in most cases they have to go into debt coming up with tens of thousands of dollars for the down payment necessary to acquire each property. It is also risky I watch them cross their fingers and hope for great tenants! There is always work involved in the upkeep of their properties, so it's not really passive income - and it can take years before they start to see some positive cash flow.

Although real estate can be a great long-term investment and is great to have in your portfolio, you can start to earn from a book within months, not years, and continue to do so without any additional effort.

The lure of passive income is one of the reasons you see very ambitious and successful people publishing books, and I can show you how to make it work for you in the following chapters.

One of my long-time author friends consistently earns $16,000-$25,000 or more in royalties each month through the books he published on Amazon.

I know this amount of money seems staggering to the average person - but let's say you only made the average amount of $400 dollars a month? How could that passive income contribute to your life? All for only 90 days of focused effort?

My friend is just one example of the countless authors who are making their living writing and publishing eBooks! The fact is, self-published authors are now making more money than all of those whose books are signed with the major publishing houses.

There is no business that I have personally been a part of that requires so little investment of time and money for such a great return. And aside from passive income, there are many other ways in which a best-selling book can bring more money to your bottom line - as well as helping you create the kind of life you've always dreamed of having.

I can promise that once you write your first book, you will want to do it repeatedly. Just imagine if you were to write one, two, or even more books a year for five years. What kind of passive income you could create over time?

Remember that most of my book sales are generated organically through Amazon traffic what this means is I put my book online and it makes money effortlessly. Whenever I choose to put in a little extra effort with marketing or events, my numbers are even greater than those I showed you. For example, in the first 3 months after I published **Visions to The Top** I made $5,261.20 by delivering 3 speeches for a sales company I approached a great bi-product of now being an authority in my niche.

When I appeared in the Huffington Post and Forbes my profits spiked upwards of $2000+ a month in sales.

I will show you how to get that kind of publicity later in the chapter 20 on marketing.

Develop the Proper Mindset for Generating Passive Income

As with any new endeavor, it is important to lay the right groundwork if you want to be successful. Usually this means developing a mindset which will support the process you're about to engage in.

Author of Rich Dad Poor Dad the best-selling personal finance book of all times - Robert Kyosaki says, to obtain financial freedom, one must be either a business owner, an investor or both, generating passive income, particularly on a monthly basis.

Always remember that building passive income is the key to becoming financially free, and that writing books can help you build this residual income. I recommend to all my clients in Self-Publishing Pro to set the financial goal of having their passive income exceed their expenses. The ability to not have to think about paying your monthly bills because you are automatically generating enough income to cover them is an amazing thing.

Start to think of writing income-generating books like planting seeds the more you write, the more your seeds will grow into rewards which you can reap.

However, just as each seed needs to be watered and given proper attention to grow, so do books. With this in mind, I will teach you how to come up with an idea that sells, how to launch your book properly, market it the correct way, and then watch your book take on a life of its own producing the passive income you've been dreaming of.

The strategies you're about to learn will help you to join in on what financially successful people do. It's well known amongst successful people that The richest people in the world look for and build networks, while everyone else looks for work. The strategies you're about to learn will help you tap into this wisdom, as you learn to write a book that builds on the idea of network and community. This will all make sense once you start to refine your book idea in chapter 8.

Focusing on the importance of passive income, and understanding the need to build a network around the book you choose to write are both essential if you want to enter this process with the right mindset.

A final word of caution, though. Writing your book with the sole purpose of making money is the wrong mindset to have. Instead, I invite you to approach your book with the intention of serving more people. When your content serves its audience, your work will stand out and the money will certainly follow.

CHAPTER 2

If Others Can Do It So Can You

Some Success Stories of First Time Self-Published Authors

Independent Consultant Becomes Best-Selling Author

Brianna Greenspan has spent most of her adult life working in a family owned business. She enjoys what she does, but wanted to find other ways to inspire and motivate people. Over the span of five years, she watched with great interest as three close friends become bestselling authors, witnessing how many people they were able to impact with their books. One day she came to me asking, "If my friends can write successful books, is there any reason I can't?"

She confided that she had a great idea about creating a coloring book for adults and kids which would include positive affirmations, but that she knew nothing about the business side of publishing. Her friends – who are also best-selling authors – and I took on the job of mentoring her through the process of writing and publishing her book *The Miracle Morning Art of Affirmations: A Positive Col-*

oring Book for Adults and Kids.

Brianna said that she loved the fact that she had accountability to keep her on track, and guidance during each step along the way. She finally felt confident enough to turn the idea she had in her mind for so long into a reality.

While fully engaged in her career, she was able self-publish in about three months.

Brianna now has a best-selling book and looks forward to publishing more by using the process she learned following the mentorship she was given.

She made over $1600 from her book in the first month and it has opened so many doors for her.

She is happy to say that the cushion of passive income which her book provides monthly has allowed her to reorganize her consulting business. Today, she delegates more so that she can focus on writing more books – providing her with the chance to do what she loves most: impact the lives of others in a positive way.

Introvert Finds Success with His First Book

At first, Matt Duncan was hesitant to even think about writing a book because he felt his schedule was already stretched to the max.

He was concerned that he wouldn't have enough time to finish his book, and when he finally decided to do it, he had no idea what to write about.

Thank goodness, he remained an active member in Self-Publishing Pro – continuing to write while he built his sustainability business.

He not only found a great book idea, "The Upcycled Toys Club: A Family Friendly Recycling Activity Series" made it to the top of the charts on Amazon.

These are just a couple of success stories from people just like you who used the system I'm about to teach you.

The people in these stories not only became successful authors, they used their books as a key to open new doors for them in business. They are pleased with the passive income which shows up in their bank accounts each month, and delighted with the lives that they can impact along the way.

We all have the same 24 hours in a day to work with. If one person can realize their self-publishing dreams, so can you. You started reading this book for a reason, and I want to assure you that you can experience the same amazing results as others. All you have to do is commit to following the strategies outlined in this book.

There is little doubt that writing a book is a life-changing experience. It changed my life, and thanks to my Self-Publishing Pro clients, I'm having the opportunity to see how much writing a book is also changing the lives of others.

Publishing a book can be a stepping-stone towards financial freedom. Maybe you want to be a public speaker, a coach, or an entrepreneur. Writing a bestselling book can be the first step towards making this happen.

Writing a book is also a great confidence booster. The success you experience by creating something worthwhile for yourself has the power to wipe out all the bad feelings you may have as the result of past failures to do so.

Successfully completing something – perhaps for the first time in your life – and watching your book become a best-seller will make you feel amazing. All of a sudden, people will want to know your story as well as the person behind it – namely, you! Once this ball is set in motion, many new doors will begin to open for you.

I guarantee that all this is possible if you follow the process laid out in this book. I have seen incredible results repeatedly, and can promise you the same kind of success if you follow my step-by-step approach.

In the following chapters I will teach you how you can become a successful author even if you've never written anything before in your life.

I will also provide the strategies for marketing and launching your book so that it is guaranteed to be successful.

Try to stay focused as I go through the Book Launch process in detail. If you continue reading to the end – I promise it will be worth it! Feel free to have your highlighter and pencil out because I want you to mark up the pages and take notes about what you're learning.

Determine Your Why

Before you start to write a book, you need to determine your reason for doing so, and make a commitment to yourself. I will be covering both of these things in the next two chapters. Try to take them seriously. A commitment combined with a sense of purpose is what will set you up for success with your book.

Write a book that people want to Read

If you want to build an income writing books then you need to focus on producing quality content that adds value to the lives of your readers.

A long time ago, someone taught me that the amount money you make will be in direct portion to the amount of value you add to the market.

So, when you start your journey, post a sticky note on your laptop asking yourself:

"How can I add value to my reader's lives?"

The #1 Rule for Writing

I'll be teaching you how to come up with an idea and decide on your audience later in the book. For now, just know that to be a successful author, you should focus on writing content that is both practical and concise, and which is easy for your target audience to read.

Writing that which is practical or useful to your audience means that its content should help them solve a problem, answer a question, or overcome a source of pain in their lives. Practical writing provides the reader with concrete solutions which can be easily implemented.

Concise writing means that you try to get straight to the point. With all the distractions of modern life, it's tough to sit down and read a long book from cover to cover. Readers want to get in, find a solution, and get out. The more concise and to the point your book is, the better.

You should also consider the fact that people are drawn to storytelling. If you can get your point across within the context of a compelling story, you book will be that much more memorable.

Finally, your book should be written in a way that is easy to read. People will overlook a lot of imperfections in your grammar and style if you have an interesting point to make, and provide content which is useful. I dropped out of college because of my dislike for writing, but as an author I felt liberated by the fact that I was not being judged for my imperfections.

Just make sure that your ideas flow smoothly from chapter to chapter - and it does help to spell correctly and use proper grammar. People will know if you don't give your book the attention it deserves. However, don't worry if you have no clue where all the commas and semi-colons go. Later in Chapter 13 I'll show you how to find an editor who can fix all your grammatical errors, and turn your book into a masterpiece.

By following these three simple guidelines you will be able to come up with a nonfiction work of art which people will appreciate. Just remember to make your book practical, concise, and easy to read and your readers will gladly give you their money and their great reviews.

CHAPTER 3

Conquering Misguided Beliefs

In this short chapter, I'll outline some of the misguided beliefs which prevent people from experiencing success in the self-publishing realm – and will explain the approach that best-selling authors use to overcome them. This is not just theory – I have tested these techniques and used them in my own book writing experience.

Once you understand how easy it is to overcome the difficulties associated with writing, you'll be able to complete somewhere between one and four books a year if you want to – all while attending to your full-time job.

Writing a book is much simpler than you think – you just need the right mindset, and a plan to follow. So why does it take some people years to complete a book while others seem to get it done in no time?

The answer lies in the fact that those who manage to conquer their misguided beliefs arrive at the finish line faster.

Everyone has misguided beliefs. They lurk in the back of your mind waiting to surface, and can sabotage your best efforts if you let them. You may have some deeply embedded negative thoughts about what it takes to write a book. These thoughts are like weeds. In this chapter, I'm going to help you pull up the weeds, and plant in their place the idea that you can write a book quickly, and that it will be easier than you ever imagined.

T. Harv Eker once said, "For us to change the fruits we must change the roots." The sooner you realize and overcome any misconceptions you might have about writing a book, the sooner you will come to believe in it as a real possibility.

I can tell you from experience that having a game plan will help diminish your fears and increase the confidence you have in your ability to write your book.

Self-belief is incredibly powerful! For this reason, I try to live by the idea that: F.E.A.R stands for False Evidence, Appearing Real, and needs to be eliminated. It needs to be replaced it with F.A.I.T.H which stands for Fully Anticipating It to Happen!

One of my all-time favorite motivational speakers and author, Tony Robbins once said, *"What's the difference between fear & faith? Both are made up. Fear is imagination undirected & faith is your power to direct imagination."*

My intention is to help you increase the faith you have in yourself by learning to direct your imagination in a way that makes it possible for you to write your book.

Let's take a look at the 5 most prevalent, misguided beliefs people have about writing a book, and talk about how you can overcome them.

Misguided Belief #1 "I don't have time, I am too busy, it will take forever."

Modern life is incredibly fast-paced, and busy. Most of us find ourselves constantly needing to get more done in less time.

We are pulled in many directions trying to meet the demands of our work, family, friends, and community. So how can you possibly find the time to add writing a book into this mix?

First let's address book length – you are probably overestimating how long yours needs to be. The reality is, for the same reasons you think you don't have time to write a book, most people feel they don't have the time to read one! The belief that to be good a book must be lengthy is incorrect. In fact, the opposite is true. Everyone is busy, and readers will really appreciate a book that gets straight to the task of providing them with the information they're seeking.

You may also believe that your book needs to be researched endlessly, and be a thorough investigation of all the facts. The truth is, people are more interested in general knowledge and solutions, than they are paying attention to a whole lot of detail.

Once I understood these things, it made it easy for me to write my first book in less than a month - despite my crazy schedule! My approach was to write it in 30 minute chunks, rather than trying to find time for marathon writing sessions.

In Chapter 10, I'll be outlining the professional 3-step method which will help you overcome your concerns about finding the time to write your book. I'll teach you how to write it quickly and easily in spite of your busy schedule.

Belief #2 "I'm not an expert so why would anyone listen to me?"

You don't have to be an expert or have the letters PhD at the end of your name in order to self-publish a book. The most important thing is for your book to create a following. If it does, others will buy it. Simple as that. To create a following you will need:

1. A nicely designed cover
2. A catchy title and subtitle
3. To make sure it's placed in the right categories
4. To choose the right keywords to optimize it
5. Market it to the right audience

I'll teach you how to do each of these things to generate the kind of following which will result in a successful book.

Of course, you also need to choose a compelling topic. One of the things I encourage clients in Self-Publishing Pro to do is go on Amazon, find a topic they're interested in, see what's missing in this category – and write a book to fill this hole in the market. I'll go into greater detail about this strategy in Chapter 7.

When I wrote **Visions To The Top** I was no expert on visualization and meditation, but I did practice both daily, and it was a subject that I felt passionately about. I simply did some research to learn more techniques, then added my own insights and personal experiences to make it interesting. It was only after the book was published and successful that I became an 'expert' in my field – sought after for interviews and advice on the subject of visualization. The same can be true for you on whatever niche you're passionate about.

Misguided Belief #3 "I hate writing and I'm not good at it."

I hear this all the time and to be straight up with you - I don't like writing either. Just so you know – I talked into my computer and had it type up the words you're now reading!

Being a best-selling author is not about being a great writer. I'm going to show you how to make your book a best-seller despite your limitations as a writer. Just stick with me if you want to start experiencing the type of freedom which comes with earning passive income.

Misguided Belief #4 "I have no idea what to write about."

If you're stuck with out an idea - I completely understand. I felt the same way before I wrote my first book, and most of our Self-Publishing Pro clients also felt this way before they got started. Just remember that we all have a story to tell, and experiences to share. My job is to show you how to get these ideas out of your head and down onto paper.

Later in the book I will teach you a 15-minute brainstorming exercise that help you see that you have plenty of great ideas. People regularly comment on this exercise with feedback like, "Justin that brainstorming technique helped me so much! I came into this with no idea where to start, but now I have so much to write about that I think I'll need to write more than one book!"

I absolutely guarantee that you will feel the same way after we go through this process together.

Misguided Belief #5 "People won't like my work."

Doubt about how an audience will judge their work creeps into everyone's mind, especially when you're spending time engaged in a creative endeavor. My mentors and other bestselling authors taught me a strategy that will help you dispel this belief, and enable you to write and market your book like a pro. Authors like J. K. Rowling, and Stephen King both use this method, which I will teach you later in the book.

The idea that no one will like your book crosses everyone's mind – even mine. My job is to teach you how to overcome these counterproductive beliefs, and lay out a plan that you can follow to take advantage of Kindle, and turn your ideas into profits. Once again, if you don't have any ideas at the moment don't worry - I will show you how to come up with some money-making ones that will excite you.

In the next chapter I'm going to explain how I came to write my book, and show you that anyone can do it. After that we'll get to the nuts and bolts of getting your book written and published.

CHAPTER 4

How I Came to Write My First Book

It feels just like yesterday that I was sitting at my desk, hand on my mouse hovering over the "publish" button on the computer screen. I was as anxious as I was excited because I didn't know what the outcome would be when I put my newly finished book out there.

Every one of the negative thoughts we spoke about in the last chapter rushed over me in a wave. Fortunately, I clicked that all important button, and to my surprise, felt an immediate release. Little did I know just how my life would be transformed by this one small action.

I was finally a published author! Just weeks before I couldn't have imagined that this would be possible. What I'd like you to know is that I arrived at this place because I was ready for a big change in my life, for something new, and most importantly – was ready to give back to the universe.

Defining Moments

Most of us have a turning point in our lives – a time at which we ask ourselves, "What is my purpose in life?"

For me this defining moment occurred on an otherwise very ordinary day. I had just finished a long day of work in sales, and was pulling into my driveway when a young man jumped out of a Red Eclipse, and started running towards me with a gun in his hand.

I could see the desperation on his face, and knew that my life was in danger so I began screaming for help. I took off running across the lawn towards my front door with him in hot pursuit. Much to my dismay the door was locked, and he stood five feet from me pointing a pistol at my chest, asking for money which I did not have.

All I knew to do was throw my hands up in the air and began repeating loudly "GOD HELP ME".

The Sustainer of The Universe answered my prayer because, remarkably, the young man simply turned and fled.

After this incident, I remained in a state of shock for several days, reflecting on how precious life is – and how it can be taken away without a moment's notice. During this time, I made the decision to change the way in which I had been living. I knew that I wanted to spend more time with my family and friends, and to make a greater contribution to the world around me.

It was a process, but over time I came to realize that helping others was something I needed to do more of.

As a child, my parents taught me that true happiness comes from doing whatever brings your heart peace. They also emphasized how important it is to treat people and nature kindly, and to find a way of giving back to the world. These principles now echoed strongly in my mind.

I knew that publishing books was a great way in which to reach out and impact a lot of people. I had several friends who had published their first books, and watched as they began to live the life of their dreams – touching the lives of others while earning a passive income.

Then one day, in a moment of reflection as I sat by the lake in my backyard, I wondered to myself, "Why don't I write a book?" From that moment on, I was unstoppable.

I spoke to friends who had published books, I read books, attended seminars, and watched as many instructional videos about self-publication as I could.

Before long I had spent thousands of dollars and hundreds of hours learning from the best mentors possible. I came to believe that if others could write a book which turned into a best-seller, there was no reason why I couldn't.

Eleven weeks before I sat at my desk to push that all-important "publish" button, I set out on a quest to fulfill my dream of becoming a best-selling author. I know that if I, and many others have done this – so can you!

I don't know if you're aware of this, but if you have any desire to write your own book there is no better time than now. We are living in phenomenal times where the Internet and social media has made self-publication incredibly easy. It is now possible to inspire people across the globe with a single book! In the next Chapter I will explain in detail why I believe that everyone should take advantage of this great opportunity to share their story and insights.

Just keep in mind that anything worthwhile involves some sacrifice. Even as a child, when you tackled that 100-piece puzzle, or assembled a model car you had to chip away at it every day. But remember how proud and accomplished you felt when you put that last piece in place? Well, the process of writing and publishing a book is the same.

The good news is, it's easy to get where you're going when you have a great map to follow. Why go it alone when you can follow a system which has a proven track record for success? The **Book Launch Formula** will serve as your guide – follow it and I can guarantee that you will come out a best-selling author at the end. You will not only create a source of passive income for yourself, but will transform your life with the many new and exciting opportunities which will result from publishing your book.

I wrote my first book after a critical turning point in my life, with the intention of serving and teaching, and it turned into a source of income which now allows me greater personal and financial freedom. I didn't set out to become a leader in this industry or someone that people could follow. I just wanted to write a book that would inspire others and get me out of my own funk. It turned out that **Visions to the Top** helped me make connections with amazing people, and opened many new doors for me. Now with the **Book Launch Formula** I am offering the benefit of my experience to my friends and clients so that they can follow or outperform my success.

If I can transform my life by publishing one book with very little talent or love of writing – so can you.

So, let's get started!

CHAPTER 5

Why Timing Is Perfect

People are addicted more than ever to their electronic devices and never has it been easier before to get your book into the hands of these people who demand instant access to information.

A main reason most people have a sort of addiction to quick information is because every time we look at our phone our brain releases dopamine and that is actually what people are addicted to. Almost every time our eyes meet our screen dopamine is released into our bloodstream. This happens because the electronic stimuli these devices put out.

In this chapter I'm going to explain to you why writing your book right now will be one of the best decisions you could ever make.

Some people think that books are not in style these days but they couldn't be further from the truth. Books have been with us since the beginning and they are not going anywhere. In today's world, these books are just going digital and becoming eBooks or audiobooks.

This all started when companies like Amazon made material more accessible through devices like Kindle. There literally has never been a better time to put your stories out there to the world. Because now people can listen and read them on multiple electronic devices and different platforms.

Do you realize that there's now over six billion people on this planet and out of those 3.2 billion of them have some sort of an electronic device with Internet whether it be Kindle devices, Android or iPads.

The question is how big of that pie do you want to carve out for yourself?

Steve Scott a very successful published author has written dozens of books because he looked at these numbers and realized this profession is a no brainer. He now makes over $30,000 to $50,000 every single month from his books.

The key to being successful is getting started, knowing how to take advantage of momentum, consistent guided effort, and never quitting.

Next time you're out at Starbucks, the airport, train, stores or anywhere people congregate look around and see how many people are walking around looking in their handheld devices.

People truly are fascinated with their devices that's why Google, Apple, and Amazon just to name a few are leading the way and maximizing this advantage of the demand for this market.

People just love to be in control of what they put in their mind, and now with the click of a button people can watch movies, TV shows, and read e-books no matter where they're at in the world.

As a matter of fact, I noticed a man reading on a kindle device at the airport and after talking briefly I asked him how he likes reading from an electronic device. He told me he loves it because it's convenient and easy to use. He mentioned he has purchased over 300 books for that one device.

It used to be that you'd have to get in your car drive to the bookstore walk up and down aisles and look through a bunch of different books to find something good to read. Today people just go to Amazon type in any word that interest them and the most relevant books sort to the top and they can buy them with one click.

And man, oh man the feeling of waking up looking on your computer and seeing that people from ALL OVER THE WORLD are buying your book while you sleep is awesome!

This will happen to you too because like I mentioned half the world is online on Amazon, Google and Apple and they aren't going anywhere. They are just expanding to new countries which means new potential customers.

One of the coolest things about this is it's absolutely free to put your book on their platform. Yep you heard me right, they don't charge anything for you to put your book online. You get to partner with the biggest businesses in the world today and you get to keep 70% profit of all the sales that happen.

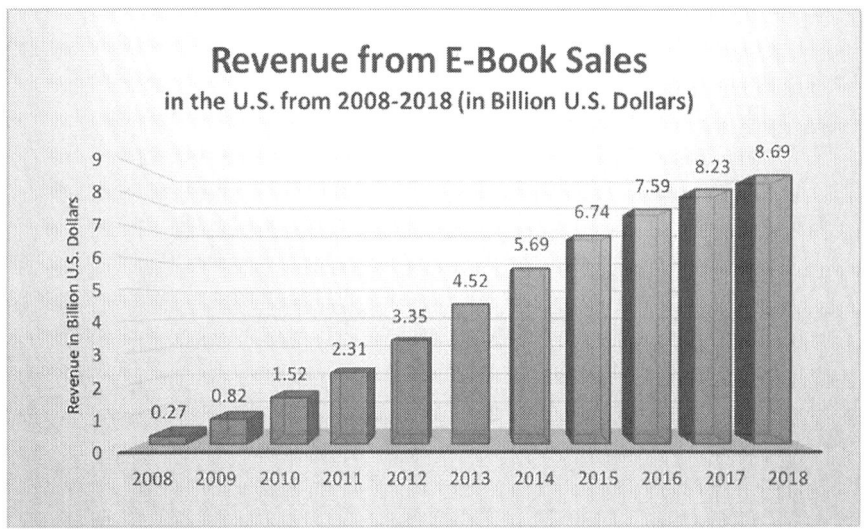

In 2012, the CEO of Amazon Jeff Bezos released that online e-books are out selling physical books. Year after year this has been the case. This is because in the last 10 years the Internet has grown by 600%.

To our benefit, research shows that over 62% of users go to the Internet to obtain information.

This will only get better with time. The latest polls show that by 2020 there will be over 5 billion users online. In 2008 for the United States alone, sales for eBooks was over 270 million dollars. Even more awesomeness, evidence shows that in 2015 people bought more than 6.7 billion dollars' worth of eBooks.

If you do the math that's over 250% growth each year!

Having your book online is like owning your own store front in every country except with no employees, and no rent. A storefront that takes very little management once it's up and running.

It's never been easier to start an online business and make a passive income. A passive income that YOU can control and that is not dependent upon other people's efforts.

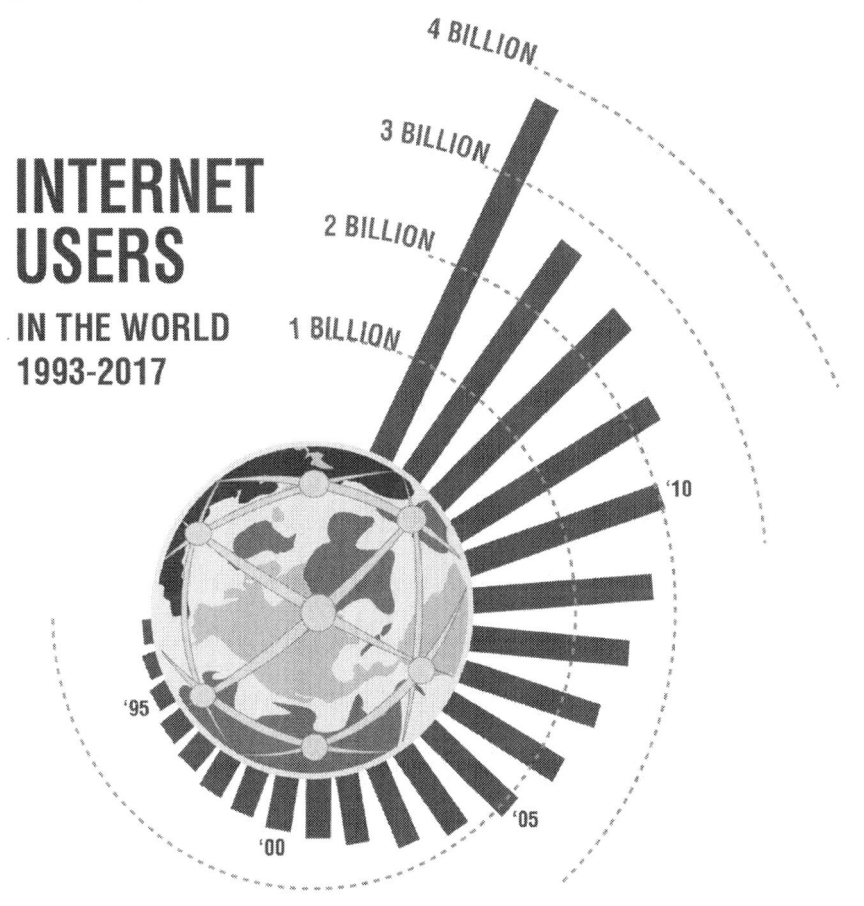

(Source: Internetworldstats.com)

I've shared with you why there is no better time to write a book, my hope is that you see this digital opportunity is growing since more and more countries and people are getting access to the Internet every day.

Marc Reklau got fired from his printing job in Germany and decided that he wanted to write a book and publish it. He was fascinated with mindset and instilling the right habits in his life so he figured why not write a book on this topic. *30 days- Change Your Habits Change*

Your Life went on to become a best seller in both English and Spanish. His book completely changed his life in so many positive ways.

My intention is that you learn from Marc's loss because the simple truth is, it is better to have a water well built before the day you become thirsty.

Writing your book is equivalent to digging your water well that will provide for you over and over again. Capitalizing on the timing of the digital movement will be one of the smartest decisions you've ever made.

If you've made it this far then you're at least interested at the different reasons why a book could help you.

CHAPTER 6

The Different Reasons People Write Books

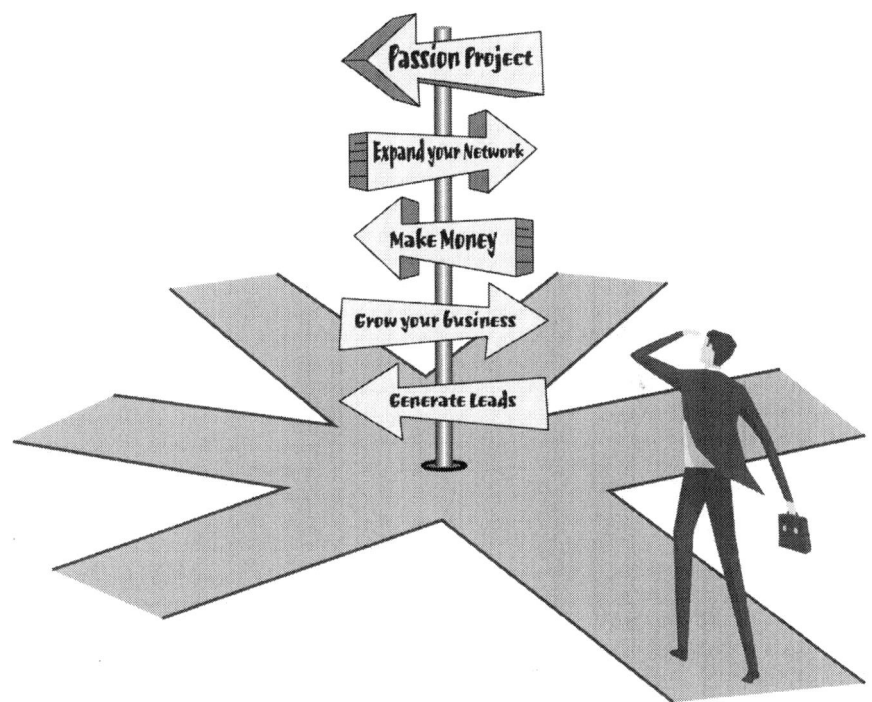

In order to make your book writing process easier, it is really important to understand your reason for writing it. It's been said when you know your why the how becomes easy. Having a sense of purpose will help keep you focused, and will make for a much better book overall.

When I wrote **Visions to the Top**, I wanted to find a way to share my insights on meditation & visualization with others, as well as to carve out a source of passive income for myself. This is quite a general purpose, but because I wrote it for a specific group of people it gave the book a real direction which made it relatively easy to write.

People write books for several reasons but there are four that weigh more than all of them. To help you have success it's crucial you define your reason for writing your book. To assist you, I have described the four main reasons people write a book:

Establishing Authority

What better way to let someone know you're the real deal than hand them you're best-selling book? Your book can act as a glorified business card – providing you with immediate authority, whereby others will view you as experts in your field. Let's say your networking and a prospect ask you a card instead you say "I don't have a card but I have my book"…

Do you realize how credible that'll make you look. If that prospect is looking to hire someone they will hire you over the dude who hands them a business card. Besides what ends up happening to business cards most the time? They're thrown away, whereas with your book it'll be put on their shelf looking at them and eventually they could pick it up to read it.

Generating Money and Leads

Writing a book can be a great source of revenue, but it can also be a way to generate leads if you are trying to build or grow a business. Just look at what happened to John Ruhlin when he wrote ***Giftology: The Art and Science of Using Gifts to Cut Through the Noise, Increase Referrals, and Strengthen Retention***

His book is filled with great information and packed with how to content. Naturally business owners who want to know how to give gifts to clients that actually produce an ROI will see him as an expert and in return some of those readers hire him and his company.

John's business generates an extra 7-10 leads a week from using this strategy.

If your aim is to generate leads and new business from your book the end goal is for the reader to contact you and hire you for your expertise. If this is your why then your book would be written in a way that at the end after they read it they will want to call you and hire you.

If you would like to write a book to grow your business the key is to load the book with amazing content that teaches the reader what they are seeking. Come from the mentality of being a giver and be very generous with how much you teach in all the chapters and in one of the last chapters you will include your call to action section.

Just remember you don't want to come across as salesy in those content loaded chapters, and keep the call to action at the end of your book. The rule is tell all the way through the book and then do a call to action in the end.

If you really pour your heart into those beginning chapters and give valuable content away generously what happens is you open your reader's mind to having a conversation with you.

PRO REMINDER: If your book is just one big advertisement people will not like it at all, they will put it down immediately, and people will see right through your intentions that you used your book as a big advertisement. Readers understand authors use books to market their products and services and they don't mind as long as you give them enough juicy content to where they could go out into the world and do it on their own.

If you want to generate leads to make more money for your business your goal in writing should be to give enough content that your readers could take what they learn and go do it themselves.

What will naturally happen is some of the readers will be so impressed they will think to themselves "I could do this myself but it'd be great just to hire the author to do it for me (or to help and make it easier)".

By using this strategy of being generous with content you open the door for that conversation and the leads will organically pour in. With that being said you will need to include a call to action chapter which will be located as one of the last chapters in your book. You can title it: Should We Continue the Conversation? This chapter will be shorter than the other chapters but will explain many powerful things and could go something like this.

1st section: Who is the Author's Ideal Customer

- "I prefer working with (insert your ideal client, then proceed to list the qualifications of your ideal client)"

2nd Section: List the Services you provide To That Niche Audience

- "These are the services that I can provide to my clients. (Insert all the services you provide)"
- Option 1
- Option 2
- Option 3

3rd Section: Set The Reader's Expectations

- "When you contact us you can expect us to (insert your introductory offer, the benefits that you promise, or how you will solve their pain or problem) "

Say it in a way that there is no surprises so they can know what to expect

4th Section: Provide How The Reader Can Contact You

- "You can reach us at (insert phone number, website, or e-mail)"

This technique works great in all industries from selling your unique products, to health and diet packages, coaching, financial services, and online how to courses. The foundational reminder is to load your book with amazing content that keeps them intrigued so they want to continue reading more.

When writing a book that will generate leads it also helps to share success stories on how your business / product / service helped others overcome their difficulties. Writing in a way that will naturally incline your reader to want to enlist your help.

The last thing I will say on this and why it works so well is because Ralph Waldo Emerson coined something called "The Law of compensation" which means when you give an abundance of information and value to people they will have the deep subconscious desire to repay you. That is the reason that at the end of the book you inform them how they can contact you to get your product, service, webinar series or whatever it is you have to offer.

PRO REMINDER: Add as much value as possible to your readers and naturally some will just want to repay you. Just write the absolute best book that you possibly can and your readers will love you and the content and the ones who can afford you will hire you and make their life much easier, and the people who don't have the means to hire you will also benefit from the book, and the good deeds you set forth will naturally come back to you from somewhere unexpected

Expanding Your Network

Having a book will help you to connect with all kinds of people: business owners, members of the opposite sex, somebody you want to do business with, other authors, podcasters, and bloggers – all of whom can help you to expand your network, in ways that would take you years to accomplish.

When you write your book, I recommend you tell almost every person you have a conversation with that you are an author. Notice their expression will be one of intrigue and interest. People will immediately connect with you because almost every person has thought to themselves "It would be so cool if I wrote a book"

They drop their guard and start asking you questions and it's like they are talking to a friend they haven't talked to in a while.

A funny example of how a book can expand your network was from a friend of mine named Hal Elrod who is a bestselling author of over 11 books. One day he was sitting in an airport and noticed there were several girls taking photos with a guy.

After looking closely Hal realized that the guy was a famous athlete for the Los Angeles Rams. Since Hal was a fan of past successes he thought it would be cool to meet him, but he didn't want to approach him like all the other fans always do.

So he thought to himself, how can I stand out and be different? Hal just so happened to have his book on him in his backpack, so he opened it up, autographed the inside cover and walked up to the man and told him he was a best-selling author and that he appreciated his talent in the game and handed him a copy of his book.

The athlete was excited and very pleased to meet him and once he looked at the back of the book and saw the photo of Hal he was open to exchanging numbers and having a new friend in his Rolodex.

You never know who you're going to meet, so once you write your book make sure to always have 1 or 2 copies on you.

A Passion Project

A person who is writing on a subject of their passion will feel as if they are in a state of flow and will be driven by that purpose

Seeing your book as a passion project can mean a couple of different things. Writing a book on something that you truly care about like a charity or something that you want people to become more aware of is one of the most fulfilling projects you can ever do.

You will feel connected to your purpose, and know this to be true when time flies by effortlessly.

Whatever your reason for writing a book, having a clear vision of why you're writing your book will make your job easier and more focused.

My wife's book, **The Rich Minimalist** was a passion project. She wanted to educate readers of the importance of living higher quality lives owning less stuff. Her goal was to imprint the idea on each reader to leave less of a carbon footprint, and some of the profits went to her favorite charities that save the earth. On top of all that she wanted her book to generate a nice passive income for our family.

If you decide to write about your passion it has the potential to become your purpose and it will give you the option of that becoming your profession.

The last piece of professional advice that I can give you on this subject is don't go into writing a book for the sole purpose getting rich quick. That puts unnecessary pressure on your back and makes your writing and marketing more strenuous.

I have had many successful businesses and I'm here to tell to how writing a book can build a small fortune for yourself. You need to see this as a long-term business and a way to create a platform for yourself.

If you come into this telling yourself I need to make 30K in the first month then you're in for a surprise. You can make that kind of money absolutely but it does take time. Instead, try to focus on your writing and know that the money will come in good time.

Follow the process you're about to learn in the next chapter and see your book as a piece of art.

Example of an Author who got connected

Before joining Self-Publishing Pro, Jenna Bayne was your average 26-year-old girl from a small town in Canada.

She didn't have anything to make her stand out from the crowd. Before writing her first book she had never written more than a short-term paper. In fact when she was younger she couldn't read until 6th grade.

Her mom introduced her to poetry in 3rd grade and she fell in love with the way it rhymed and flowed. These poems are what helped her to learn how to read.

One sunny day many years later in Cleveland, Ohio while running a trail with Jon Vroman, the creator of the Front Row Foundation, an incredible foundation that gives terminally ill people the chance to live a front row experience for one day before they pass away, Jon asked her "what is your greatest love and your greatest fear?"

Jenna said "I really love giving hugs and writing poetry and I truly fear speaking in public".

Jon responded with "once you align your greatest love and deepest fear as your life work is the moment you will begin to live your life in the front row.

Fast forward a couple years…

When she told her friends and family that she was going to write a book in 90 days everyone doubted her. Most people told her that she couldn't write and publish a book that fast.

This just motivated her even more because she knew if others could do it so could she. When people said it wasn't possible she became more motivated to prove them wrong.

Like the saying goes "They hate us because they ain't us," these comments just lit a fire under her to get to work.

Despite her fears she signed up for the Self-Publishing Pro program. Up until the program began, she carried the constant doubt, instigated by the people closest her, that she would never achieve the promised goal: being a #1 bestselling author.

She not only wrote her book but started without even having an idea for a book, to launching it in just 12 weeks.

Since publishing her first book, she feels that she writes with greater purpose. She has helped people and had more impact than she ever imagined possible.

She never had a guided purpose for the words she was putting on the page before joining the program. Now she's writing with purpose and direction.

Jenna loves children and really wanted to impact them in a positive way, especially to teach them the importance of self-confidence, how to overcome self-doubt, how to love their body as it is, and how to care for the environment.

Originally, her purpose was to write stories from her life with the hopes to come to an understanding of how much she had grown and changed. She soon realized that her story had bigger meaning than just writing a book; it was to help change the lives of children around the globe.

Her passion for poetry shines through her work and her rhythmic approach with words are captivating to children and parents alike.

She never would've guessed that she had this skill but she listened to her inner voice and reflected on that conversations she had with Jon on that sunny day in Cleveland, Ohio.

Since writing her first children's book, numerous parents and children have said how much of an impact her writing have made in their lives. She now speaks at conferences and on podcast regularly and even though she still has the fear of public speaking it has dwindled down.

Because like we teach all of our members at Self-Publishing Pro, everything is challenging until it becomes easy. The best part is she gets to fulfill her passion of writing poetry and most importantly giving lots of hugs to her readers and listeners.

Because of this passion project her self-worth has increased, her confidence flies sky high, and her book has had a positive impact on her social, financial, and academic life.

Her book has been downloaded over 3,000 times, and she continues to be asked to speak to adults and children about her book, ***I Am Part Of Nature.***

The individuals who take action and join our Self-Publishing Pro community are able to follow a proven path. A path that gives them new and exciting opportunities, and allows for unexpected abundance to arrive in their life.

Jenna is now in the process of finalizing her second book and she is a perfect example of what I mean when I talk about having a clear purpose for your book.

We helped her in our own little way to realize her true potential so that she could be the change she wishes to see in this world.

ACTION STEP:

Grab a pen and paper and write all the different reasons why you want to write your book. Set a timer for 15-30 minutes… Ready… Set…GO!

**Setting a timer is a tactic we teach to help to intensify the activity and will 100% without fail help you to get things done faster with more precision. I'll explain why this productivity hack works so well in a little bit in the next chapter.

When writing your purpose try to be as clear as you can, knowing that this will provide you with a direction – but also with the clarity you need for marketing your book.

If you don't know where you are heading before you start to write your book, it will be difficult to get there.

Just before you're ready to start writing your book, write down your reason on a sticky note and put it on your laptop/computer to reinforce your purpose.

CHAPTER 7

4 Ways of Creating a Book Idea

Phase 1

In this chapter I'll be helping you to figure out what your book will be about, even if you don't have the slightest idea what to write about.

Perhaps you have a subject which interests you, but you need to clarify the focus of your book.

Whatever the case, don't get too bogged down with this task, it's actually fairly easy to narrow down your topic once you understand how to approach it.

In the last chapter I asked you to think of why you are writing your book – now it is time to focus on the what.

The best way to figure this out is by doing a free-writing exercise, in order to have your brain connect to the ideas you already have inside you.

Technique #1: Free-Writing Towards an Idea

The free-writing process is a great way to help you hone in on a topic for your book. This exercise will allow you to ask yourself, "What will my book be about?", and for 10 minutes without stopping jot down every idea that comes to mind.

When you do this exercise keep your goals in mind and reject nothing at this stage. Literally write down every single idea that springs into mind – even if it seems random. Remember, whether you're aware of it or not, you've probably been thinking about this book for a long time – and you'd be surprised at how much your brain processes without your knowledge!

Your mind is actively working as you attempt to fall asleep at night, while you're taking a shower, waiting in line at the supermarket – these ideas are just waiting to find their way out and onto paper, and this is their chance!

Your only job is to write fast enough during these 10 minutes to make sure you get all these ideas down on paper! Just write whatever comes to mind.

Step 1

In order for brainstorming to be effective, it is important that you time yourself. We get more done when we have set deadlines. Be sure to set a timer.

Step 2

Ask yourself "What sparks my interest – gets me really excited?"
We all have something which we feel passionately about, and which intrigues us. Find your spark! Think about a topic you enjoy learning or reading about that you dive into without being forced to.

Step 3

Still not sure where to start? Use these 3 categories as a guide: topics of interest, experiences, and job related.

Topics of Interest- This is something that gets you excited when you think about it, you don't have to be in love with this subject, just something that you have a curiosity about. Finish these sentences on pen and paper or on a word document:

"I'm interested in…"

"My hobbies are…"

"I've always wanted to write about…"

"The reason I want to write a book is…"

"My favorite topic is…"

"I know a lot about…"

Experience- You don't have to be an expert on a topic just have experience with it. Finish these sentences:

"I have experience in…?

"I can definitely teach people about…"

"My experience allowed me to learn…"

"My unique personal experience was…."

Job Related- is tied to past experience and lessons learned at current or previous profession. Complete these sentences.

"When I worked at _____ I learned about…."

Or

"In my profession I know a lot about…"

"I want to be known as the leading expert in…"

"The one area in my business people to need to know about is…"

"I could write a book related on the topic of my business because…"

"If I wrote a book on… I could impact more lives…"

"My experience working in (insert profession) could teach people more precisely about…"

"Since I worked in (insert profession) people would be benefit on my knowledge of…"

The most important thing is to keep writing, not filtering out anything which springs to mind. If you can't think of anything, write about not being able to think of anything! Don't worry about grammar, or spelling – just keep writing until your time is up.

If you're still writing at the end of 10 minutes, immediately set another timer for 10 minutes and allow your flow to come to an end naturally.

Some of you will see results from this free-writing exercise, ending up with an idea which can now be refined.

Others people may not have been as successful, and still have no direction for their book. If this is the case with you, it's time to consider approaching this task from a different angle.

Technique #2: Use an Aspect of Your Business to Generate an Idea

If you really want to be identified as an expert in your field you can write a book that is alignment with your business.

Let's say for example you are a physician and you have two different ideas for your book.

The first is about "Stories from past patients" and the second is "How to avoid a heart attack".

Both would be good options because this physician has interest in the subject, multiple past experiences, and there is competition on the market in Amazon.

I must say if this physician wants to be identified as "The Expert" it would be wiser for him/her to write about the second topic.

Because in media, and press releases it would say "Dr Shalaby best-selling author on the topic of how to avoid heart attacks" which would give this doctor more authority than stories from past patients.

For this scenario a key technique to maximize your outreach is by using your network of doctor friends for testimonials and endorsements and recommend that they refer their patients to you. Past clients would be happy to leave positive reviews on this book and from that it would be given "Amazon Juice". An extremely important piece of the formula we will discuss later in chapter 17 "Launching Your Book The Pro Way".

If there are 5 heart physicians in a zip code it likely that none of them have ever written a book. Writing a book tailored to specific niche in your profession will make you stand out as the go to authority and will allow you to DOMINATE that niche because people will see you as the person they should hire.

Not to mention open doors of opportunity for paid speaking gigs and being hired as the leading consultant. It's important to note that choosing this idea over writing a book on stories from past patients will give this doctor multiple advantages in his industry and make him/her shine as the leader on that specific topic.

Whatever the result of this free-writing exercise is for you, I suggest that you now go to the Amazon Kindle store in order to browse through the top books in categories which interest you.

Technique #3: Use Amazon to Find an Idea

If the free-writing exercise failed to generate an idea for you, consider writing in one of the four categories which always sell well in Amazon.

If the topics of books in any of the follow categories interest you, start to think of this as a direction for your book:

- Health and Fitness
- Relationships
- Time management
- Stress Management
- Money Making Strategies

You will notice that each of these categories are "self-help" – directed at solving a particular problem in one area of life. They are geared towards physical or mental well-being, managing daily living, or finding financial freedom.

If you choose to allow one of these categories to be the jumping off point for your book, try to keep the following in mind:

Take note of themes which are common to the bestsellers in each category. For example, if juicing is a common theme in different sub-categories of diet and fitness, that means that it is trending. Consider trending topics – in this case juicing – to be a greenlight. You always want to write about a topic which is popular.

Rather than thinking that there will be no need for another book on a trending topic – that it won't sell – take this as evidence that you have an idea for a book which will be in popular demand. This helps you to see that people are actually paying money to learn about it.

We could spend 2 hours explaining how to find an existing market and capitalize on that but since this is your first book that is not necessary. All you need to know is go to Amazon, type in a keyword on a subject and if you see it has around 15-20 reviews then that's means there is a good chance people are buying for that niche.

Remember competition is a good thing because that shows you people are interested in that subject. When I first started out in sales I read multiple how-to books on sales just to learn from people experiences and to find jewels of wisdom through multiple perspectives.

When coming up with your idea have your intention to create an impact in this world and the content that you write will reflect.

Technique #4: Use Reviews to Get Ideas

Read the 2 and 3 star reviews of the bestsellers in the category of interest to you. Use this feedback to help you find a direction for your book – you can provide readers with what they felt was lacking in any given book.

Using this strategy, you can find an idea for your book with a minimal amount of effort. Once you find a topic you think you can write about with passion, spend a weekend looking for a void which you think needs filling in that niche.

Take a close look at the bestseller ranking for books that are trending. You should know that a bestselling book ranking lower than 20,000 is selling several copies a day – which is great!

By using these four techniques you will be able to find your book idea. Have fun with this strategy and see how many ideas you can get on paper because in the next chapter we will refine these ideas so you can get started on your book!

CHAPTER 8

Refining Your Book Idea

Phase 2

Regardless of how you settled on an idea, I am now going to show you how to refine it even further. This means taking a general idea, and making it more specific. By participating in the last chapter we can now turn those ideas into a more specific target.

You are about to learn how to dive deeper by doing research on Amazon, use reviews as a tool to make your idea even better, and how to niche down to a specific group of people who will want your book. Here we go.

The process of refining your idea will help you connect even more with your topic. So let's say you selected "Stress Management" as the general topic in Phase 1, in this phase it's about going deeper and making it more precise to a specific group of people.

It's been said it's better to know who you want your customer to be, then aiming for everyone. Your goal is to identify a target audience and by doing so this will allow you to be successful with Amazon. How you do this is by going a mile deep and only an inch wide, not the other way around.

When digging for gold, oil, or water you have to dig deep to hit the target otherwise the efforts are wasted. The same applies for you being specific on exactly who you want your audience to be for in your book.

For example instead of just writing a vague book on the category "stress management" you'll notice several specific subsets of this topic that are doing pretty well.

- A Guide to Living More Present
- The Art of Mindfulness
- Declutter Your Mind

By diving deeper you are niching down from a vague idea to a specific idea. You need to target a group of people and solve their problem.

To do this: Go to the bestseller section in the Amazon Kindle Store, and look for books written on topics which line up with your idea.

Assess the length of books similar to the one you want to write – maybe your category is in need of a shorter, more concise book!

Look at the table of contents inside the bestselling books – is there anything missing? Read the book description, and pay attention to the comments of readers. The comments people leave are where SO many answers are at. You can refine your idea just by reading from the comments section of other related books.

Technique #1 How to Use Reviews to Refine Your Idea

When you are reading reviews have your investigator hat on because you can learn exactly what people want, or exactly what people disliked. This vital information should be noted and added in your book.

Positive Reviews- Tell you what the readers enjoyed and took away from the book. Scan through the 4 and 5 starred reviews looking for:

- "What I liked most was…"
- "The most valuable lesson was…"
- "The author did a great job…"

For example I just read a 5 star review for a book on "How to stop worrying" and the reviewer said they really enjoyed how the author taught how to breakdown our patterns in life from thoughts, life obligations, relationships and surroundings. She mentioned how breaking it down like that was easier for her to understand than other books.

So from that little bit of research I immediately came up with a book idea on a similar topic "How to overcome anxiety in 4 simple steps"

I didn't dive any further than that so I'm not positive it would be a successful book, but in 30 seconds of reading reviews I got an idea based on positive feedback from one simple review.

If you spend more time on this task of reading comments from related books you can come up with great ideas by finding patterns in the market. These patterns will help you to refine your book topic and make it what readers want.

Negative Reviews- I would even argue these reviews are better because you learn how the reader was disappointed by the author. You can take that pain and make it your gain. Scroll through the 2 and 3 star and look for comments such as:

- "I didn't like how…"
- "This book didn't have…"
- "This book was missing…"

These type of comments will help you to quickly evaluate what's needed for your niche. For example after reading 2 and 3 stars on a book about Spicing up your marriage, I learned a lot of things. The readers stated they wanted more techniques and ideas on what activities to do with their spouse. They also said they wanted stories from real people.

So within a few minutes of browsing I came up with the idea of writing a book on keeping your marriage fresh: 7 activities to spice up your marriage. Again not sure if this would be wildly successful, but you get the idea.

PRO TIP: Click on filter button and select all positive and all critical reviews to save yourself a ton of time. Otherwise you will be reading reviews for days. This trick will allow you to only the see the most popular reviews voted by the public.

Seeing what buyers are saying in their reviews can really help you narrow your focus. Try not to get bogged down by perfection – remember how crippling this can be! Maybe you feel that you don't have the perfect topic for your book, but you can always refine it further as you go along. The key is just to start writing ideas on paper, and mentally commit that you will come up with your great idea.

The clearer on who you are targeting the better. It is said riches are in the niches. So avoid going after a broad audience and add more traits to target specifics.

Technique #2 Refine Your Topic Towards A Specific Audience

Example 1:

[Vague Audience] First time authors

[Specific Audience] First time authors want to write non fiction

Example 2:

[Vague Audience] How to lose belly fat

[Specific Audience] How to lose belly fat for women over 40

This will make your readers self-select themselves, which is what you want. By selecting exactly who you want to write to you carve out your slice of the pie.

Pinpoint the objective/benefit

Example 1:

[Vague Audience] Learn how to swim

[Specific Audience] Learn how to swim in 10 easy steps

Example 2:

[Vague Audience] Learn Coding

[Specific Audience] Learn how to make money coding without leaving home

By digging a little deeper and really establishing who you want to target this will benefit you in multiple ways: First your readers will enjoy the book more because the topic is precise and talks exactly to them.

Second you save a lot of time writing because you'll know exactly who you're writing to. Lastly it will just be easier for you because you'll have laser focus on your target.

The key is to find your audience's pain points and explain to them the solution. People buy nonfictions books to solve their problems. When you're refining your idea aim to look for a group of people that you can share your perspective with and offer your solution.

I have a friend who is a heart specialist and wants to write a book. Writing a broad book about hearts would be much to general. After a quick conversation I learned the most common reasons why patients visit him is to learn how to prevent cardiovascular diseases.

I then asked him what age range and gender these clients fell into, and he said that 75% of them were male and between 55-65 years old. That conversation was golden because he realized that was super targeted and would sell.

"A book that teaches people how to prevent cardiovascular disease for men over 55 years of age"

There are more ways to refine your book idea but honestly they are not necessary. You can find a great idea by using technique 1 and 2. The most important thing is to take action and start writing notes on paper.

ACTION STEP:

Determine the "outcome" of your book in one to two sentences by filling in the blanks.

- My book will help (Insert specific Audience) with (insert the outcome)

First Example: My book will help (salespeople and entrepreneurs) with (using visualization and meditation to become more productive and manifest their life dreams)

Second Example: My book will help (First time authors) with (writing their first nonfiction book around a full time job even if they don't know how or where to begin)

It's totally fine if your statement is longer and not as precise. Keep narrowing it down until its precise. As you can see in my first book I combined two audiences. Knowing what I know now I could of wrote two different books.

One for salespeople and one for entrepreneurs. Don't make the same mistake I did and merge these into one book. It will be better for you keep the niches separate and publish two different books! It's all good because I live my life with the motto of failing forward and to keep learning from my mistakes. I recommend you adopt this philosophy.

Being done is way better than aiming for perfection but never finishing. We will teach you how Facebook uses this philosophy to this day in chapter 12 to help you get your book done fast.

Once you implement technique 1 and 2 in this chapter and refine your idea to a specific audience you are now ready to start writing. In the next chapter you will learn a strategy that will help you to create a best-selling title and subtitle that hooks your readers.

CHAPTER 9

Creating a Bestselling Book Title and Subtitle in 7 Easy Steps

PHASE 3

It may not make sense to you to be talking about creating a title for your book when you've only just refined your book idea. Just bear with me, and I promise that you'll soon understand the importance of coming up with a winning title early on.

Having a winning title for your book is incredibly important. You will learn certain strategies that will help to make your title precise and speak directly to your given audience.

Coming up with a great title for your book requires that you see the big picture and understand what you need to include in it. Otherwise, it will be like putting together a piece of furniture without instructions.

Most of you already have all the pieces which you need in order to create a title and subtitle for you book. You have a refined idea, an increased belief that you can do this, and confidence from this guideline – now we just need to craft a title which will draw your target audience in.

I have put together a 7 step process for helping you to come up with a title for your book – by understanding who will be buying your book, and more importantly, why they will buy it.

1) Figure Out Who Your Target Audience Is

Ask yourself what ONE person would instantly benefit from the content you share in your book. Try to be very precise in pinpointing who your target audience is.

Then, ask yourself how much the people you are writing it for will benefit from your book. You want to narrow your focus for the greatest impact rather than striving for a greater reach.

Examples of bad book titles:

- "The Relationship Repair System"
- "How to Escape Debt"
- "Addictions"

These titles are weak because they are much too general, with keywords which are not well optimized.

Examples of good book titles:

- "Facebook Marketing: 25 Best Strategies for Using Facebook for Advertising, Business, and Making Money Online"
- "Meditation: Simple Meditation Techniques to Get Rid of Stress, Anxiety, and to Feel Happy Now"
- "Declutter Your Mind: How to Stop Worrying, Relieve Anxiety, and Eliminate Negative Thinking"
- "The Millionaire Fastlane: Crack the Code to Wealth and Live Rich for a Lifetime"
- "Manipulation: How to Recognize and Outwit Emotional Manipulation and Mind Control in Your Relationships"
- "Project Management: A Quick Start Beginners Guide For The Serious Project Manager To Managing Any Project Easily!"

You will notice that the first word in each of these titles is the primary keyword, which insures a higher ranking in Internet searches. When Kindle readers see titles like these, they can identify with a specific claim, and are made aware of exactly what they will learn in each of these books.

2) How will your book benefit readers?

The benefits you list in your title are what will sell your book. Be precise and feel free to make big promises in your book title and subtitle – just be sure you deliver the goods in your book!

Remember – people enjoy buying books that provide them with an opportunity for transformation.

PRO TIP:

Make a long list of all the benefits your book will provide, and include as many of them as possible in your title.

Example:

Visions to the Top: A Millionaire's Secret Formula to Productivity, Visualization, and Meditation. The How-To Guide for Entrepreneurs, Salespeople and High Achievers for Wealth Creation & Dream Fulfillment

The title of my first book successfully pinpoints a specific group of readers, and lets them know that they will learn how to use visualization and meditation to live a dream-fulfilled life while increasing their wealth.

3) What benefit will attract the most attention from your audience?

Take a look at the long list of benefits which your book will provide, and spend some time narrowing it down to a few which your readers will notice right away.

When deciding which benefits to choose, try to remember that most people are more concerned with eliminating pain and problems than anything else. Make sure that the benefits you settle on are those which target your reader's primary pain points.

Then, make a list of the benefits included in your book which will address these specific issues.

Take a look at the title from my first book, which I included as an example in Step 2. The benefits included in the title speak directly to entrepreneurs, salespeople, and high achievers and are bound to capture their attention.

4) Set a timer and make a list of 21 titles

Now that you're getting a sense of the big picture, set a timer and get ready to jot down a list of 21 titles.

Try not to overthink it, just write what comes to mind even if they sound silly – you'll be picking the top 3 when you're done.

You will probably find yourself coming up with variations of similar titles, and this is fine.

5) Be Specific And Make BIG and BOLD claims.

You're probably on the right track to creating an amazing title and subtitle, but it will need a little more refining to hook readers. They need to have no doubt that this book is for them. Your goal is to make them stop browsing and click on your book to learn more.

It should be expected that you need to add a little punch to your title and subtitle at this stage – to give them, and your book, the final push it needs.

This will take some careful thought, which can be a little frustrating. Just remember – diamonds are made under pressure!

Try making your title even more specific, and the claims in your subtitle even bolder. Remember – an amazing sounding title won't sell your book if it is vague.

I have found that going straight to members of my target audience for a brainstorming session can offer a fresh, new perspective. This is something you might want to try.

Your final choice of title and subtitle should take your breath away – don't stop until it does!

Example:

"Discover Your Purpose: Focus Your Efforts on Work You Feel

Passionately About" may sound great, but it is vague. The final title choice, "A Purposeful Life: Quit Working at What You Hate and Start a Small Business You Love", is much better because readers know exactly what they will be targeting in order to find a purpose driven life.

When you're done, pick your three favorite titles, and get feedback from friends, and family and or your niche audience. You can even post them on social media to see which gets the most favorable response.

We'll touch on this later in this chapter under evaluate your title even more. Make your title one of which when your prospective clients clicks on your book cover they are intrigued to want to read your book description and introduction.

6) Creating a Subtitle

Now that you've chosen a great title, it will be much easier to narrow down your subtitle. You've probably even been thinking about some in the process of coming up with your title.

Your title should not leave readers wondering what specific issues your book targets. Now it is the job of the subtitle to let them know the benefits they will gain in dealing with the issues of interest to them.

Your subtitle should tell the audience what they are going to learn.

With my first book ***Visions to the Top***, the subtitle clearly indicates that readers will be focusing on wealth creation and dream fulfillment.

7) Choose keywords which increase optimization

At Self-Publishing Pro, our students have access to tools, software, and mentors to help them choose the best keywords for their book.

The word "keyword" basically refers to what potential buyers type into the search bar in order to find the type of book they're looking for.

The problem is, many writers try to work backwards when creating their title – beginning with a list of keywords and trying to fit them in.

Never start with your keywords in mind! Instead, go through the process step by step, just as I laid it out for you. When you're done, you can optimize your title with keywords.

In fact, if you have come up with a great title and subtitle and feel that by adding keywords gives them less kick – don't add them! It is much more important to have a killer title than to have one which is loaded with keywords.

Example:

"Laser-sharp Focus: A No Fluff Guide to Improved Concentration, Maximized Productivity, and Fast Track to Success". This title is amazing because it is specific, and compelling – with a title and subtitle which are both keyword heavy. It has incorporated the keywords "Laser-Sharp Focus", "Concentration", and "Maximized Productivity".

The subject of keyword research is so vast and we could spend hours on this alone, so we won't be able to dive into a ton of how to details here. You will find many websites and tools online that have plenty details on this topic.

Just Google "Amazon Keyword Tools" and tons of resources will pop up. When trying to find how often a keyword is searched I personally like to use KDP Rocket. As for doing Google keyword research I like to use Keyword Planner Tool.

In short, when you go upload your book on Amazon you will be given 7 blank boxes to choose your keywords. Choose the words that are relevant to your title and subtitle and that are getting searched frequently on Amazon and Google. For example when choosing keywords for ***Visions To the Top: A Millionaire's Secret Formula To Productivity, Visualization, and Meditation.***

Inside KDP Rocket I noticed there was less competition for visualization than for productivity and meditation. So my keywords I chose were based around the topic of visualization and in return my book is one of the first books that pops up when you search the 7 different keywords I selected for Amazon.

If you have done everything that is listed above picking good keywords can really help you overall organic reach. The idea is choose keywords that are being searched several times a month and ones that have little competition.

Lastly if you are writing about a specific industry and everyone in that industry uses the same jargon or speech then you don't have to worry too much about the keyword research.

PRO TIP:

Post your top 3 favorite titles on social media in order to hear what people have to say about them. Bear in mind, your target audience is your best source of feedback. Your sister and mom may tell you how wonderful a title sounds, but take their praise lightly. Instead – head straight to your end customer and get their opinion.

YOUR END GOAL is to write a few titles and subtitles that grab your customer's attention, tell them what the benefit is, tell them exactly who the book is for, and include a handful of related keywords.

Evaluate Your Title Even More

Phase 4

Believe it or not selecting your title and subtitle by yourself can be challenging so it doesn't hurt to seek guidance from your friends, family, and colleagues.

Just keep in mind that you will get your best advice from people who are considered your audience because mom and dad are going to tell its great no matter what.

ASK A STRANGER OR COLLEAGUE

This technique will feel awkward and you won't want to do it at first but the feedback you will receive is extremely valuable. Strangers provide brutal honesty and they will tell you straight up because they have no ties to you.

If you're at the tire store, or grocery checkout, or at a retail location start a conversation by saying something like this:

> "Hello!
>
> How are you? This might seem a little strange, but I am an aspiring author and I was hoping you could give me some feedback. I am writing about (Insert Topic).
>
> Specifically I need a little help choosing the title. The first title I have in mind is:
>
> (Insert title #1) and the second is (Insert title #2).
>
> Which title do you think will attract (insert your specific audience) better?
>
> From there a casual conversation will start, and you can get a lot of valuable feedback for the refinement process.

If this is out of your comfort zone you can always do the easier approach by using social media. Below is a template you can use (feel free to modify)

Facebook template

> Hey Friends — I need your help!
>
> I am writing a book about (insert topic) and picking a title by myself is harder than you think… So I want to leave it in your hands. Which do you like better?
>
> (Title & Subtitle A)
>
> Or
>
> (Title & Subtitle B)
>
> Please feel free to share your enhancements and suggestions!

FEEDBACK CAN BE PRICELESS

The main reason you are doing this is to get validation on your title and learn if you need to refine or make it better.

If people are excited and enthusiastic about one then you know that is your winner but if people are confused and not intrigued on your title now then you know they won't be responsive later.

Some best-selling authors say it's best to form you title and subtitle early on while others say you can do this after the writing process. It is your choice. I believe it's a good idea to do this task now before you put a lot of effort and energy into drafting and writing your book.

Let's recap the first four phases

By doing the first 4 phases first you will make the writing of your book much easier and seamless. These phases are crucial you complete before writing because they lay the foundation for everything else. So make sure you use them as a guideline towards your success.

Here is a quick summary of those four phases.

In phase 1 we covered 4 techniques on how to come up with a general book idea. Those included using the freewriting process, listing your interest such as things you have experience in, going to the amazon store, and using a job related topic. Whichever you feel the strongest about go with that one.

During phase 2 we refine the general topic you choose in phase 1. You do this by selecting a specific niche or group of people. Pick an audience and the end result you want to teach them.

You can browse similar books on amazon critical review section and learn a lot from positive and negative reviews. Your main objective here is to write your outcome sentence. An example is: "My book will help (Insert specific audience) with (Insert the outcome) this will make you narrow in on a niche market. Remember riches are in the niches and this will allow you to write a short concise book.

Phase 3 will guide you in writing your title and subtitle, one that grabs your customer's attention, tells them what the benefits are, tells them exactly who the book is for, and includes a handful of related keywords by using **KDP Rocket**. You craft this by using the "outcome sentence" from phase 2.

Create several combinations of your title and subtitle. Your title should be anywhere from 1 to 5 words so that people will remember it, and the subtitle will be longer (from 4-20 words) and elaborates the title

Lastly is phase 4 you will pick your 3 favorite title and subtitle combinations from phase 3 and evaluate them even more. Do this by asking strangers, colleges, and using your social media. Use this feedback to help you refine your title and subtitle even more until you come up with the winning combination.

After you decide on your title and subtitle you will move onto the next section of this process which is outlining your book. I've written two books now and I've tried both ways. I came up with the title first before writing, as well as came up with the title after writing.

It's really just a personal preference, don't be afraid to be flexible and tweak your title. Remember your title and subtitle act as a compass towards exactly who you're writing to and what their outcome will be.

CHAPTER 10

Brainstorm to Outline

Despite what most people think, writing a book does not have to be a difficult, painful process.

In this chapter I'm going to talk about the Professional 3 step method I used to write my first book, which was 130 pages long in which I completed in less than 3 weeks.

But before I lay out my step by step system for you, let me share the story about how I went from being an awful writer to publishing my first book.

Not only was I not great at it, I absolutely hated the thought of writing when I sat down to write my first book.

When I studied business in college I dreaded writing papers, and got C's on most of them and most of the time just ended up paying someone to write them for me. That skill of delegating works just as well in Self Publishing, but only if you follow this process I teach you in this chapter.

I remember a long time ago when I was in college, while most of my friends were getting A's on 5 page papers which they knocked off effortlessly in a couple hours, I struggled for hours to churn out a short paper which usually earned me a C.

Sometimes I would stay up all night, spending hour upon hour writing a short 2 or 3 page paper for classes.

I had no idea what to write, or how to write it. I can still remember the feeling of wanting to bang my fists on the keyboard out of frustration. I would even enlarge the text and increase the spacing size to help me through the agonizing process of writing. I wish I would of known then what I know now because what your about to learn will help you breeze through the process of writing.

I'm sure you're starting to understand that the rules of self-publishing have completely changed the game.

You no longer need to invest in between $50 - $100K learning to write well in order to publish your first book. I am living proof that you don't need to be a great writer or even graduate college.

So why is it that some people make writing their first book their new year's resolution year after year and never get around to it, while others grow their business by writing a bestseller in just a few months?

I've spent years figuring out the answer to this question. Those who jump in and do it understand the secret to successful writing.

I'm going to share this secret with you right now. Earlier I mentioned the Professional 3 step method I used to write my first book. So let's jump right in and take a look at the first step.

Step #1: Make Your Mind-map

The first step to writing a successful book involves brainstorming.

This really just means dumping the contents of your brain onto a piece of paper in order to create what I call a mind map.

Start with a blank piece of paper and write either your book topic - or the rough idea you have for one – in the middle of the page.

Then begin writing everything that relates to your topic randomly – all over the page. I mean EVERYTHING you can think of!

Continue writing in this way for 15 to 30 minutes – before you know it your paper will start to look like a flowchart, or one of those tree graphs from high school math class! Circles and lines everywhere.

Creating a mind map is actually really easy because you are just jotting down every idea that comes to mind – no matter how crazy you may think it is.

When you brainstorm like this you will find that you come up with so many things you might never have thought about, or would have forgotten to include if you'd just started writing.

This will save you tons of time later on. Trying to create a mind map on a computer or laptop will not produce the kind of result you're looking for.

Be sure to do it using a pen and paper. Your final product might look something like these examples below!

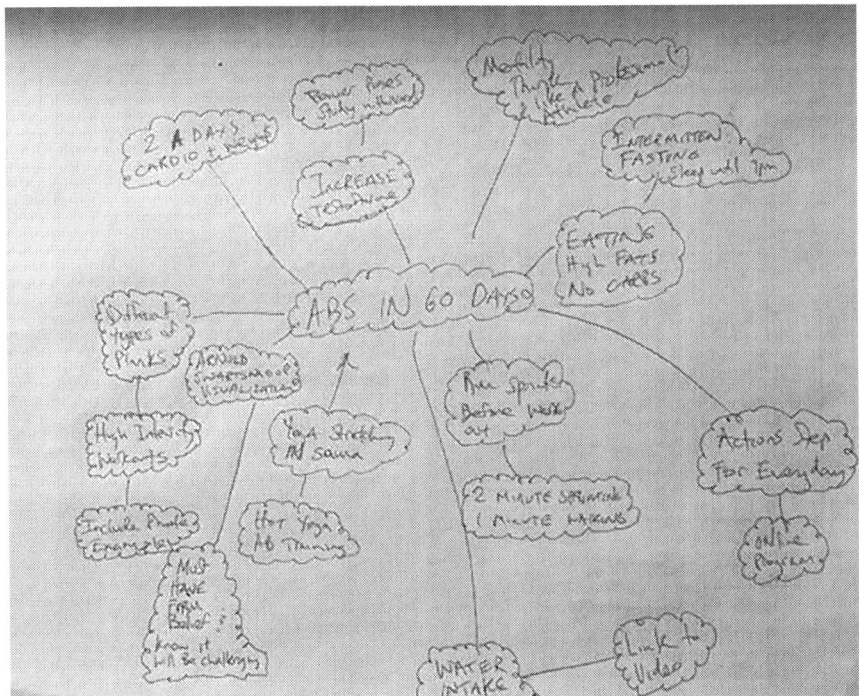

QuickNotes
Minimalism
Quality not Quantity
Personal Development
Early Retirement
Investing
more time
Personal Experience
Saving money
Less Stress
Creativity
Save Environment
Problems of Hoarding
more freedom
- less time organizing stuff
- don't have to worry about losing stuff or taking care of a lot of things
Travel
Mindset
Health
Fulfillment
Charity
Passion
Clutter free
Clean
Less binging
Cook meals
- healthy

Different Breathing Techniques
Yoga Breathing
SEE
HEAR
FEAL
Increases Focus
Guided Visualization
Types of Visualization
Multiple Images

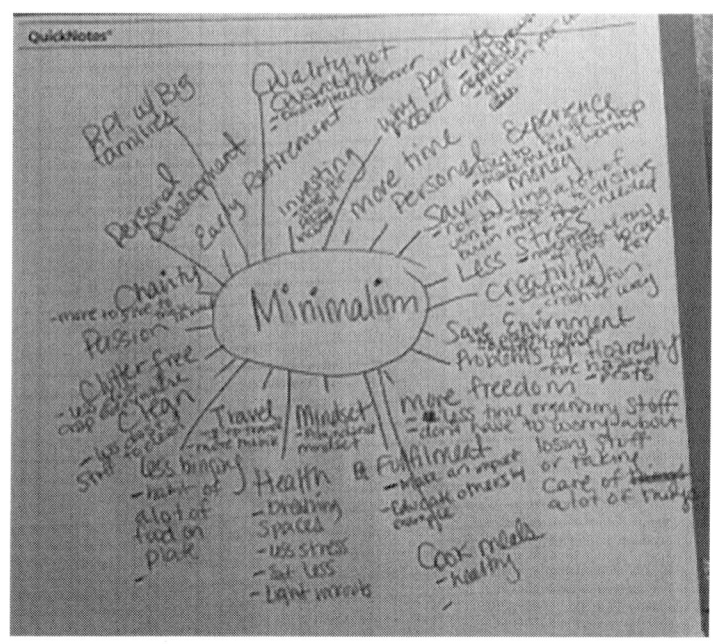

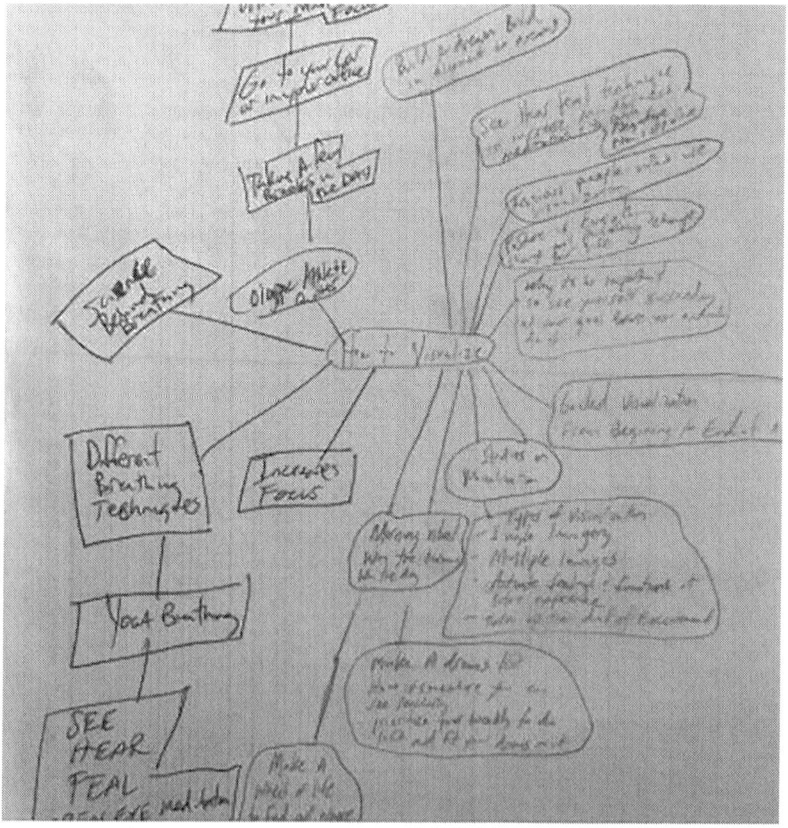

Step #2: Create Your Outline

Once you have done a mind map, creating an outline is easy.

You will start by taking common themes from your mind map and organizing them into sections.

Then, take those sections and break them into chapters. Finally, organize the chapters into an order which makes your book flow well. Think of your outline as a working table of contents.

Here's an example of what my outline looked like for my second book "***Book Launch Formula***."

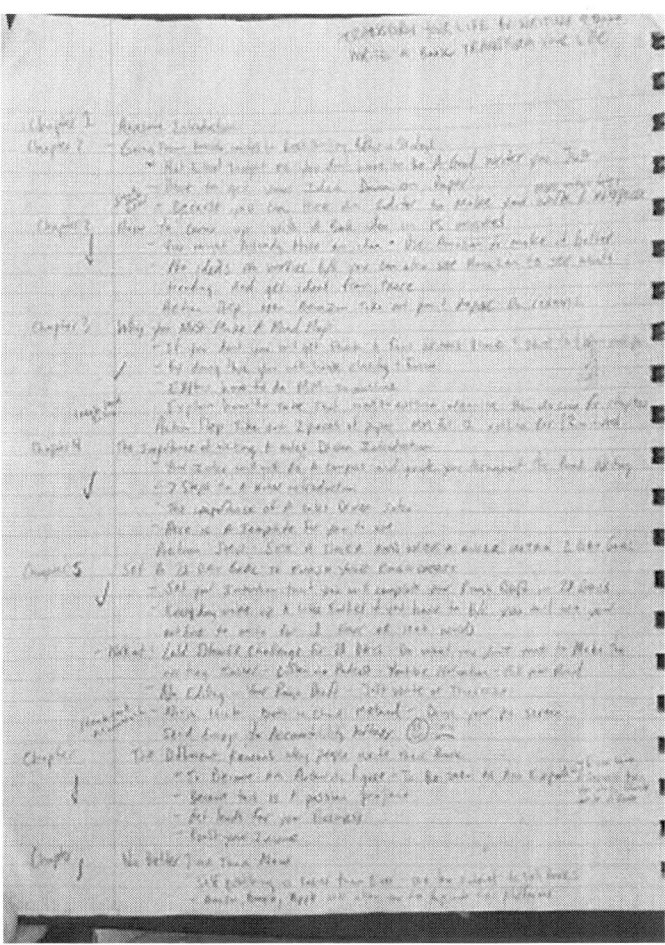

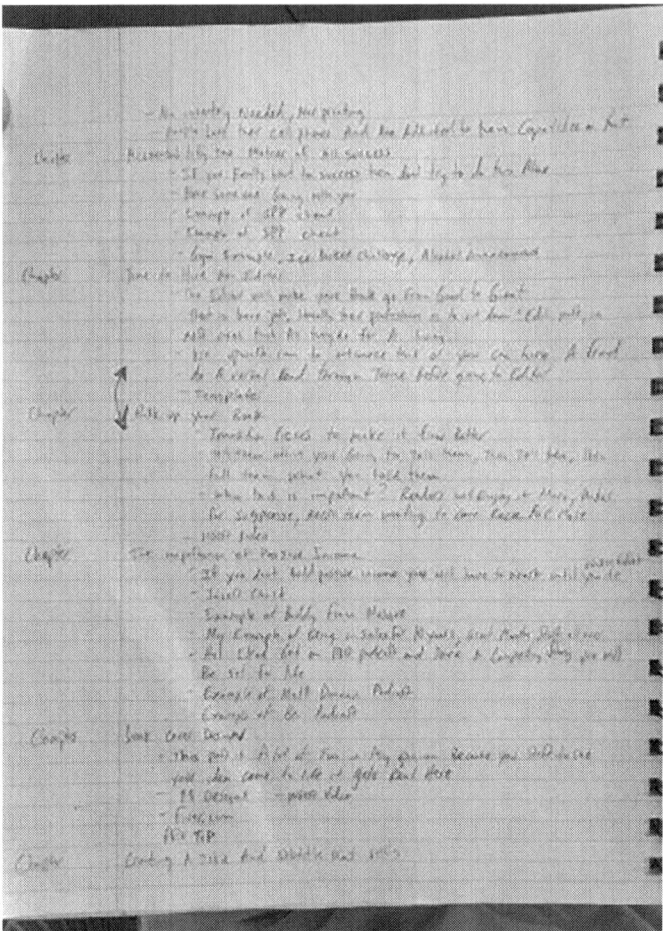

Creating an outline can be done on a piece of paper, a dry erase board, or a word document. Personally I like to hand write it. Trust me when I say you need to get this task done. It will help you big time.

Get your outline done and then take those sections and break them up into chapters and organize them into an order that works for your book.

The cool thing about this process is that it's not overwhelming. Instead of thinking about the whole book, you're focusing on a bunch of pieces which will be put together in the order you choose and we will tweak later on.

By making a master outline to follow as your road map you will be able to write your book so much easier like I did in 2 and half weeks.

Remember – your outline doesn't have to be perfect. It is just providing a framework for your ideas so that you can finish your book by moving from one chapter to the next as quickly as possible.

You will find that once you start writing, more ideas, examples and stories will pop into your head. Just add them to your outline and keep moving.

Step # 3: Start Writing

This is the final step in the process! Most people start writing without the benefit of the solid vision your outline will provide.

Those two steps are crucial before you write. The people who skip them – soon become overwhelmed and throw in the towel.

This won't happen to you, because you've laid out a great framework for yourself, and when it comes to writing – you know exactly what to do.

No writer's block – no agony of staring at a blank computer screen with no direction!

You feel confident because you're not focused on writing an entire book. You're just following your outline, writing one chapter at a time.

Now I'm going to explain the process which I want you to follow for writing your first chapter.

In the same way that you created a mind map for your book, spend 11 minutes making one for each chapter.

When that's done, spend another 11 minutes generating an outline for this chapter based on your mind map.

Finally, spend 45 minutes to an hour and a half writing the chapter, based on the outline you created.

Repeat this process for each chapter. This process may seem a little strange at first, but as you get into it, you'll find yourself in a state of flow.

You will probably find yourself getting faster at it as you go along, and before you know it – your book will be finished.

With this easy professional 3 step method, writer's block will be a thing of the past. You will just show up to write, and chip away at your outline each day.

You will know exactly where to start, exactly what to write, and how long to spend at it.

You will not waste any time – when you finish one chapter, simply move on to the next. All you have do is follow your outline.

This is the exact process I used when I wrote **Visions to the Top** chapter by chapter in two and a half weeks. Just as a reminder, for each chapter make a mind map, and use that mind map to create an outline for the chapter.

In the next chapter I will teach you the 8 steps that work like a charm to help you write a sales driven introduction that grabs your reader's attention and makes them buy your book.

CHAPTER 11

Writing a Sales Driven Introduction

The next step to take is to create a sales driven introduction for your book.

The goal is to write an introduction that hooks your readers. If they like the content in this section they will most likely buy your book. To many authors write their book but skimp out on their intro and make it boring and dry.

This section should literally lure your reader in and capture your reader's attention from the very first page. You do this by addressing their problem and reminding them of their biggest challenges that come their way.

In this chapter my goal is to provide you with a template for how to write an awesome introduction that you can use over and over again. Once you become a best seller once you're going to want to write another book I promise.

Your introduction will lay the foundation to exactly who your book is written for and completing this task will make your writing easier.

So I thought it'd be a good idea to provide you with an example so you can see what this looks like in action.

I have added examples from my first book, **Visions To The Top** for each of the 8 steps. To get the best use of these examples, check out the book and follow along as you go through the 8 steps.

Before we get going, for anyone who might not already know – on Amazon, your introduction is available for people to read when they are deciding whether or not to purchase your book. After your book cover, it is the first thing they look at. For this reason, it is critically important that you write an amazing one by following these steps.

Step 1: Identify the Problem

You want to bluntly state the problem you're addressing in your book from the very first sentence. State the problem clearly, so your readers know why they need your book to help them fix it.

For example, I wanted readers to know from the very start that **Visions to The Top** was going to be a book about productivity and dream fulfillment.

Example:

"Are you tired of logging twelve hour days, sacrificing your home life and any other dreams you might have, only to feel that you are no further ahead than you were a year ago?

Step 2: Present the Solution

Once your readers know what your book is about, you need to be specific about how you're going to help them solve the problem you've identified.

Example:

"You will learn what lies at the root of success, and the science behind cause and effect. You will learn how to be happier and more balanced, while building an abundant life free from constant struggle and difficulties. You will learn how to work smart instead of hard – no longer trading all of your precious time for average outcomes."

Step 3: Assert Your Credibility

Next, you have to let people know why they should trust you. This is your first step towards building the relationship with your readers which will continue throughout your book.

Example:

"Rising to the top in all of my endeavors afforded me the opportunity to talk to countless others who have also achieved greatness. What I learned from my experience and that of others is that it is a fine line that separates those of us who are average from those of us who end up at the top of our game.

Step 4: Re-State the Benefits

Make sure your readers are clear about what solutions you are offering them.

Example:

"Whatever you're calling in life, you will benefit from the strategies and techniques which have allowed me and countless others to generate the kind of success most only dream of."

Step 5: Provide Proof

In this part of your introduction, provide your readers with testimonials they can relate to.

Example:

"Jacob, a successful entrepreneur from Texas says, "The techniques taught in this book are exactly what helped me break records in my industry. Most of the time I can see results the same day I use these techniques."

Step 6: Make A Promise

Make sure that your readers understand that you are promising them something, and that you plan to deliver. This is another important way of connecting with your readers on a personal level.

Example:

"I promise that if you follow the steps in the pages which follow, you will not only realize your biggest dreams faster than you imagined possible, you will actually work less in the process. I promise that the results you achieve will allow you to live more intentionally, freeing up time to focus on what is really important to you and your future."

Step 7: Tell Them Not to Wait

Now it's time to let your readers know that they will be missing an amazing opportunity if they don't get a hold of your book now.

Notice how I've used repetition to drive this point home. This is a time honored way of motivating readers to buy and read your book IMMEDIATELY.

Example:

"Don't be the kind of person who has dreams that will never come true. Be that person who achieves what they think is their biggest dream, and then moves on to one that is even greater. Be that person who amazes everyone who crosses their path. Be that person who leaves others wondering how it's possible to get so much done in so little time. Be the sort of person who is motivated to take action without hesitation."

Step 8: Call Your Readers to Action

You want to entice readers to buy your book and start reading it the minute they've finished the introduction. You can do this by peaking their interest without revealing too much.

Example:

"The visualization and subconscious programming techniques and strategies you're about to learn have been tested and are proven to create lifelong results… The steps set out for you here are simple, and the results are available to anyone who is prepared to put in the work.

Scroll up to the top and Click Buy Now."

Now it's my time to make a promise. I PROMISE that if you follow these 8 steps when you write your introduction, your reader will be sold on buying and reading your book!

In the next chapter I will teach you everything you need to know to write your book quickly. I will go over 12 techniques you can follow to get your book done fast and efficiently.

CHAPTER 12

Start Writing & Finish Your Rough Draft ASAP

In this chapter we will go over the importance of getting your rough draft done as fast as possible. I'm going to be giving you the 12 strategies that I've learned from best-selling authors and that I personally use myself.

Inside Self Publishing Pro we request our students to follow our 90 day calendar because it acts as a to-do list each and every day on exactly what needs to be done.

This avoids the question of "what do I need to get done today?" By following it you are guaranteed to finish your book in 90 days.

To download our Best Selling Author 30 day Write-A-Thon template go to ***https://www.self-publishingpro.com/blf-free-resources*** .

Tip # 1 - Schedule Consistent Writing Time

Regardless of the time of day you decide to write, consistency is everything. Write at that same time each and every day.

We've already established that you're going to get your book written by chipping away at it piece by piece. Letting yourself off the hook by missing a day opens the door to missing others – and before you know it, you'll be way off track.

Being consistent leads to greater confidence, as you observe your ability to follow through on the decision you've made. It also eliminates the need to make a daily decision about whether to write or not – which can sap your energy.

When you're consistent, there's no decision to be made – you simply get up in the morning and start writing.

To those creative souls out there who think: "I can only write when I'm inspired", I'll rest my case with the following quote:

Someone once asked Somerset Maugham if he wrote on a schedule or only when struck by inspiration. 'I write only when inspiration strikes,' he replied. 'Fortunately it strikes every morning at nine o'clock sharp.'" So if you decide to write at 8am, write at 8am every day.

Don't make the mistake of thinking you can do your writing on the weekends only. It's better to take 30 minutes a day x 5 days a week than 2.5 hours on Saturday.

Your creative juice will keep flowing if you chip away a little bit every day, but if you try to do it once a week on the weekend, it will be harder to pick up where you left off. By writing consistently every day you will strengthen your mental muscle so make sure to schedule it like an important meeting you must attend.

I keep referring to 30 minutes but keep in mind that is the must do goal, or minimum goal. If you feel you like you're on a roll and want to keep going then please do.

These burst of energy come and go and you really should take advantage of them when they arrive.

Tip #2 Give Yourself A Hard Deadline Of Completing Your Rough Draft

The power of a made up mind is extremely powerful. Instead of saying "I will try to finish my rough draft in 30 days" I want you to change your words and say "I will finish my rough draft in 30 days."

Follow Master Yoda's teachings "Do or do not do there is no try". So it is crucial that you set your intention and take action every day to accomplish completing your rough draft by your deadline.

You can and will complete your rough draft if you use the professional 3 step method regarding your mind map to outline for each chapter.

Using this system, each chapter took around 2 hours to write and even less time to talk and have my computer dictate. I'd repeat the process again with next chapter every morning before work, and before you know it I had my rough draft done.

As the result of practice, my writing became better and more efficient with each chapter. Before long 2 hours were reduced to one and three-quarters, one and a half, and finally one and a quarter.

The lesson here is – the more you write, the faster you become.

Tip # 3 Write in the morning

You might be saying to yourself "ahh I'm not a morning person" and I completely understand because I used to feel the same way, as well as several of our clients, but what they found is the morning time is when our minds are most fresh and haven't had to make tough decisions yet.

You will find that you will be more creative, more focused, and once you do it a few times it will become a habit. I even recommend to first-time authors to drink a cup of coffee or tea.

Own your morning, don't let it own you! To many people rush out of bed and out the door to work. My schedule is just a demanding as others since I run 2 companies, but for 90 days I made up my mind that I would turn off the TV at night, or get off social media, go to bed earlier and wake up earlier and spend 30 minutes minimum on this life changing project.

Tip # 4 Put Yourself on a timer

Always put yourself on the clock – literally! Consider downloading a timer app on your computer, or access a free timer website. Having an alarm go off will keep you moving, and works much better than trying to "guesstimate" your start and stop times.

This strategy comes from Parkinson's Law which states "work expands so as to fill the time available for its completion" and basically what this means is you get stuff done faster when there is urgency. When you have a timer set, you'll notice an intensified sharp focus to complete the task at hand.

Tip # 5 Keep Writing!

Starting to write can seem like a daunting task – but it is imperative that you put your fears aside and start writing as soon as possible.

Always remember to focus on the process of 'writing' in the loosest sense of the word. Just focus on getting words down on paper in order to complete your first draft.

It doesn't matter if what you write is good, it just matters that you're writing! As I said in the previous point your writing will become better and more efficient with practice– but it also became higher quality.

Remember you don't have to be a good writer because the editor is the one who will make your work great!

Tip #6 Don't edit as your write!

This advice is priceless and was given to me by Honoree Corder, a 19-time best-selling author. The best authors just follow their mind map and outline, just put the words on paper, and don't go back and edit because it will stop your creative flow.

I made the mistake of not listening to this and after writing a paragraph spent way too much time going back and editing. It feels good to chip away and get content on your document.

Even if there is misspelling, bad grammar, or content mistakes it doesn't matter.

We will come back to it later and clean it up. The key is to get your rough draft done. This little hack will make your writing **WAY** easier and more fun. You will get more done and feel better because you accomplished more each day.

It's perfectly normal for your first draft to be a mess, nobody is going to read it except you. Allow yourself to fail forward by not trying to make your rough draft perfect.

Remember done is better than perfect. In the next chapter we will show you how to give your draft to a professional editor who will make your work shine bright.

Tip #7 Block All Distractions

With a deadline of 2 and a half weeks, I knew that I would have to remain very focused when I started to write my book. In order to do this, I tried to minimize the distractions, and the first thing I did was power off my phone.

If you want to write efficiently, you should also consider turning off computer notifications, and even disabling your Internet. Creating an environment which is free of distractions will help you get your book written in record time.

Whatever chunk of time you seal off for writing – make it a sacred commitment.

Whether you decide to write… 1 hour, 2 hours, or multiple hour chunks… Set a timer and write for exactly that long. Force your block of time and stick to it.

All I ask is your commitment for 30 minutes to 1 hour of focused writing per day. If you can't be off the grid for whatever length of time you decide on, you might want to take a second look at how you've chosen to live your life.

30 minutes x 5 days a week is 2.5 hours throughout the week. Even if you're a parent, or overworked, you can find a way to squeeze 15 minutes in the morning and 15 minutes at night if you absolutely have to. Shortening your lunch break is an option as well. 5 minutes here and 5 minutes there is better than no minutes at all.

This is a short term blast of effort that will transform your life for years to come.

Tip #8 Stay Inspired through personal growth.

Writing your book requires your commitment and focus. Ultimately if our mind is being fed with inspiring thoughts it's easier to stay the course. So I recommend on your way to work only listen to inspirational information such as podcast, TED talks or YouTube videos.

You can actually generate incredible ideas from listening to others on your given topic. When I was writing **Visions to the Top** I used the technique of listening to powerful content everyday on my way to the office and when I arrived I would jot down notes of ideas I picked up.

Tip #9 Write Down All Your Idea Right When They Come

Once you start on the journey of writing your book, your subconscious mind won't stop until it's done. So it's important to be ready when ideas come to you, because they will.

Some of your best ideas will come out of the blue when you least expect them. Make sure to jot them down anywhere you can. I had a writing pad in my car, a notes section in my iPhone, at the gym I remember even asking for pen and paper to write the ideas that popped into my mind, once noted I went right back to my workout.

Keep the ideas brief, a lot of times it was just one word or a few words. When I arrived to writing mode I put those ideas in my outline in the right place.

Tip #10 Have Some Accountability (Set Specific Goals & Deadlines):

It is vital that you have someone hold you accountable for a set of clear goals and deadlines. This is arguably one of the most important rules of all.

Not only is the kind of self-discipline required to write a book hard to come by – it also requires a lot of your precious energy. This is why it's essential that you find an accountability partner.

A good accountability partner will help keep you on track. They'll be there to keep you focused when you feel like giving up. And, because they are going through the same process, they'll make you feel less alone in your challenges.

When working with new aspiring authors we always pair them up with someone that they can be accountable to because in life and in business distractions come our way and it's our way of guaranteeing that each member stay on track.

Make sure to have your Commitment To Yourself printed out and hung up where you plan on doing your writing. Just seeing this document will keep you inspired to finish your goal.

Tip #11 Let Your Voice do the typing

Our clients at Self-Publishing Pro say this is one of their favorite ways to overcome writer's block and to get a lot of content on paper. In this section I will share with you my favorite strategy to really getting a lot done.

All you do is have your organized outline in front of you and have your Google Docs open, click on tools, and then click voice typing.

From there you will read one sentence at a time, then move onto the next sentence in your outline, until you finish all that you have written down.

Then go back up to the top sentence and talk about that as much as you can into your computer. Repeat this for each sentence and before you know it you'll have the whole chapter done.

Talk in a casual tone as if you're explaining it to your friend. Once you're done with your rough draft then go back and edit as you like.

Bonus Tip #12 Exercise and Take a Cold Shower Each Day

I know this might sound out of place but working out and taking a cold shower during your writing stage will give you the mental strength you need to stay focused. It has been said how we do anything is how we do everything.

When we do difficult task that we don't want to do we become stronger mentally, and our mind becomes stronger so that we can push through anything.

We have an optional cold shower challenge with the members in

Self-Publishing Pro and our clients dread this at first but after a few days they love it.

According to research, taking cold showers instead of hot showers provides surprising health benefits for our mind and body — from burning fat to depression relief.

- Increases Alertness. ...
- Refines Hair and Skin…
- Improves Immunity and Circulation…
- Stimulates Weight Loss…
- Speeds Up Muscle Soreness and Recovery…
- Eases Stress…
- Relieves Depression…

Again, this is optional but the "crazies" who participate in our community love it and say it helps them in their life in many ways not just writing.

Quick Summary

These twelve tips you can implement immediately will help you write your book around your full-time schedule. These are techniques that some of the biggest authors in the industry use and they worked for me and can work for you.

These are all helpful but the most important of them all is tip #1 to schedule consistent writing time. The reason being is it's important to build the habit of putting your butt in the chair because without that it'll be difficult to write your book.

CHAPTER 13

The Different Stages of Editing

Stage 1: The Three Phase Revision Process

Many first time authors make the mistake of thinking that revising and editing are the same thing. Nothing could be further from the truth.

You are about to finalize your book and send it off to your editor, but before you do this you need to read it through OUT LOUD, so that you can get a sense for how it sounds and flows. This review of your own work is called revising.

When you revise your book, your attention should be focused on hearing how it flows, and seeing if it makes sense. The goal is to get your book as close to its final version before you hand it over to an editor to work their magic. We'll be talking about how to hire an editor a little later in this chapter.

You want to catch the little things which an editor might miss – they are not mind readers and can't possibly know what is most important to you. Revising your book before handing it to an editor will allow you to double check and make sure you emphasize how you want the book to flow.

PRO TIP:

Make sure that your review process consists of reading your book OUT LOUD. This simple step will help expose so many errors, and enhance the quality of your work.

Your verbal read-through will help you unearth:

- Awkwardly written sentences.
- Phrases that don't flow, or transition well.

- Grammatical errors and typos.

The more you find, the less your editor might unintentionally miss.

Divide your revision process into the following three phases:

Revision Phase 1:

Read your book objectively – from the vantage point of a stranger. Look at it through the critical lenses of an outsider. Ask yourself the following questions:

- Do the words flow off my tongue, or are they difficult to read?
- Is the language precise?
- Do some parts require more detail, and should I remove some from others?
- Can an outsider easily understand the point I'm trying to make in each chapter?
- Do I transition smoothly from one idea to the next?
- What are my favorite parts in the book, and how can I make the others as amazing?

Revision Phase 2:

In this phase, you will be analyzing the structure of your book.

Ask yourself the following questions:

- Does the promise which I made in the introduction get addressed as a main focus in each chapter?
- Are the chapters of your book well organized, and presented in an order which makes sense?
- Where can I add supporting links that connect chapters?
- Does my book go full circle - do I have a great conclusion which ties everything together?

Revision Phase 3:

In this last revision phase, you will be evaluating your voice. New writers often find this very difficult. You want your personality to shine through your words – otherwise it will read like a boring textbook. Nobody's got time for that.

Books which are written in a conversational tone, and are easy to read are just as believable and persuasive than those which are written in "academic language".

The key is to be sincere in your writing, and keep your target audience in mind.

ACTION STEP:

Read your book OUT LOUD, imagining that you are an outsider seeing it for the first time. Focus on the structure of your book. Try having someone else read it to you, while you make revisions.

Make sure that your voice is what you intended – that your personality is present in your words. Otherwise it be super lame and boring for the reader.

Find as many typos and grammatical errors as possible. Now that you've revised your book, let's get it sent off to an editor as soon as possible!

The next few sections will focus on how to bring a great editor on to your team. I will be talking about not only the editing process, but how to keep an editor on time and on budget.

Stage 2: Quick and Easy Editing

Can you sense how close you are to finishing your book? Now that you've completed your first draft, and the revision process, we can move on to the process of hiring and working with an editor. Once you've completed this section, your book will be ready for publication!

In this section, I will go over how to easily hire an editor and keep them on track, as well as the different types of editing. This process does not have to be expensive, and should only take a couple of weeks.

Just keep in mind that "done is better than perfect". Facebook uses this motto to push out new ideas and products and I recommend you adopt the same philosophy. Trying to perfect your work will bog you down and not allow you to publish.

Push through the editing process without worrying about perfection – preserving your strength for the launch.

A Bad Writer Turned Great Because of Their Editor

I have already told you how I grew up strongly disliking writing, and never considering it to be one of my strengths. However, when I completed *Visions To The Top* I hesitated to send it off to an editor – worrying that I needed to make more revisions before it would be ready.

This was a mistake, and I encourage you to learn from it. Send your book to an editor as soon as possible, and let them work their magic on it.

I was tempted to hold on to my book after going through the revision process twice, but thank God I didn't. Once I found an editor and put my book in her hands, she was able to make tremendous improvements to it.

Don't worry if, like me, you are not the best writer – your editor will make you a great one! Your job is to find someone with solid reviews and experience, and they will turn your book into an awesome read.

Give yourself permission to hand your book off to an editor as soon as possible, so that they can do what they do best!

The 2 Types of Editing

There are essentially two types of editing: content editing, and copy editing. You should know this, but don't need to worry about it – this is the job of your editor. Before we get into the difference between the two, as well as how to find a professional editor, I want to clarify a few key points.

Solid content is what counts on Amazon and Kindle – your readers will happily forgive a few grammatical errors if the content is there. Editing won't make your work perfect, just more readable.

Your book will NEVER, EVER be perfect. Set a deadline for yourself or the editing process will never end

To this point, several years ago I met with a customer of mine to go sharpen her CUTCO knives and I told her about the success of my book. We talked and she told me that over 4 years ago she started a book and never finished it. I asked her why and where she dropped the ball and she told me she tried to do it all herself. Meaning she had no team, no accountability, with no deadlines, and where she slipped was she got bogged down in the editing process and quit somewhere along the way!

She's not the only one I've heard this from. The key is to set a deadline in editing phase. The editing process should take somewhere between 2 – 3 weeks, and no more.

You will notice that all 4 of these points relate to what has become our motto "Done is better than perfect". I want you to set daily goals, moving steadily towards the finish line. If you fail to do this you will be fixing, tweaking, perfecting, and over-viewing until you start to see your first grey hairs.

Content Editing

In this phase of the editing process you and/or your editor will be looking at the big picture – the content of your book. You should be asking yourself questions like:

- Does my book flow – is it an easy read?
- Are there parts which need more detail?
- Do sections or chapters need to be moved around in order to make more sense?

- Can I get rid of some things to make my message more precise?

- Are some parts of the book unclear, needing simplification?

- Are there gaps in the book – things which need to be included to make my message clear?

- What can be done to make my book even better, and add more value for my readers?

Some of these things will be addressed in the revision process, as you read your book out loud. However, your editor will be a truly objective reader, seeing your book from an outsider's perspective.

Sometimes things make perfect sense in your mind, but you aren't able to get them out of your head and onto paper in a way that makes sense to others. For this reason, multiple perspectives are crucial – get as many as possible and take a serious look at the feedback you get.

Copy Editing

Once your message, or content is clear, your editor can really take over and make a big difference to your book.

Even if you're an amazing writer, I don't recommend overlooking an editor as you go through the process of copy editing. In this phase of editing, your editor will fix spelling and grammatical errors – but will also make your book more compelling.

Your editor will probably need to rewrite portions of your book to make it more precise, correcting word usage and repetition.

Even though content is king, copy editing is extremely important – too many spelling or grammatical errors will take the focus away from your message.

PRO TIP:

As you go through the editing process with your book, don't worry about formatting. It will change after each edit, so save this until the very end after your final edits have been made.

In the next section, I'll show you the easy, step by step process of finding a great editor for the right price – so you can just sit back and see your work come to fruition. Hiring an amazing editor is one of the keys to your success.

Stage 3 Finding an Amazing Editor

I know from personal experience that trying to find an editor for the first time can be a daunting experience. Anytime we do something new, it seems difficult until we move past it.

In this portion of the book, I will hold your hand throughout the process of finding an amazing editor to work with you on your book. I recommend that you hire an editor for both content and copy editing, but the choice is up to you.

Locating the Talent

When it comes time to hire an editor, you have a couple of choices.

Hire from within your own personal network – someone recommended by a colleague or friend, or hire from a freelance website.

Hiring from within your own personal network is self-explanatory. Just make sure that you can rely on the feedback you've been given, and be sure to be clear about deadlines and payment procedures.

I know several writers who have found a great editor from within their own personal network. It is possible to find some amazing talent from within your own circle of influence.

PRO TIP:

Consider the smartest person in your English class, or a favorite English teacher to be great candidates.

If you decide to hire from a freelance website, the following section is for you.

Hiring on Upwork

Upwork is an awesome network which is easy to use. I have hired several skilled professionals, including editors, on this site.

Simply head to www.Upwork.com and set up an account following the easy directions.

Once your account has been set up, click on "Post a job". Select "Name your job" and enter:

> "Editor needed for_____".

Fill in the blank with the genre of your particular book, for example "Editor needed for self-help book".

Upwork Job Description Template

Then, simply copy and paste this EXACT text in the description section:

> I am looking to hire a skilled professional with English and literary skills to edit the content, and copy edit my book.
>
> My book has already been revised a few times, but needs a final edit before the book is published on Amazon in the next few week.
>
> My book is a ____ book that talks about _____.
>
> I am on a fairly short deadline, so I need someone who can be focused and work quickly on this project over the next 3 weeks.
>
> The copy and content edits must be completed by ____ (insert date 3 weeks out).
>
> My book contains _____ words, _____ chapters, and _____ pages in length.
>
> I am looking for an experienced editor who has an interest in this topic.

You should know that I am working on this book with best-selling authors, so this will be a great chance to get more exposure for you and your editing work.

I will be requesting a short 3 page sample edit of your work.

If this job interest you, submit a proposal telling me why, and quoting your best price. Also please include the word "Juicy Mango" at the top of your proposal.

If you have any question, please let me know.

Be sure to provide editors with information about the topic of your book in the descriptions section. For example, "Mine is a self-help book that teaches readers how to maximize their productivity, and use visualization and meditation to create the life of their dreams."

Also, be sure to communicate the importance of your deadline and need for someone with focused attention. This is essential if you intend to find someone who will stay on track.

Finally, decide on a budget and stick to it. You'll notice prices vary with different editors I suggest that you be prepared to pay $0.005 - $0.016 per word. So, for a document that is 23,000 words it'll cost around $115 and $368 for this editing job. Use this as a rough estimate, and remember you can always negotiate and settle on an amount, and on someone you're comfortable with.

PRO TIP #1

To weed out freelancers who are bidding randomly on every job, at the end of your posting you should make a request that candidates include a certain word at the beginning of their proposal. I tell them to include "Juicy Mango" as the catch word and the ones who do not include this I don't even consider because they didn't take the time to read through your entire job posting. You can change it to any fruit or word you want. Just so you know, juicy mangoes are my favorite fruit.

PRO TIP #2

Consider uploading 3 pages of your book as an attachment and ask serious candidates to do a sample content and copy edit of it, to be submitted with their proposal.

PRO TIP #3

Be sure to select the correct category to post your job in. I recommend you choose "Writing and Translation" as your primary category, and "Editing and Proofreading" for your secondary category.

Once you post your job, just sit back and relax – in a matter of hours your inbox will be flooded with proposals.

You will naturally gravitate towards a few proposals. Focus on these, checking candidate's reviews and success rates. You may also wish to schedule a Skype interview with those who are of particular interest to you.

ACTION STEP

Regardless of whether you decide to hire an editor online or through your personal network – make sure you do it as soon as possible. Schedule start and finish deadlines, and stick with them.

Do your research, and be confident in your choice. Trust your gut, and hire away!

In the next section of this chapter I will give some hints about how to avoid the pains of hiring a bad editor, and tell you how you can keep your job on track and on budget.

Quick Summary

By following the 3 stages of editing exactly how I listed them you will thank yourself later. The 3-phase revision process, quick and easy editing, and finding an amazing editor will allow you to breeze through this process saving you time, energy, and money. By using this as your guideline your books content will flow smoothly, you'll hire a professional editor who does this for a living and in turn your manuscript will turn into a work of art.

No One Has Time for a Bad Editor

Thank God I've never had the experience of working with a bad editor, and neither have any of my clients at Self-Publishing Pro. You obviously don't want this to be part of your experience either, and it won't as long as you choose well and lay out your expectations from the start. As well as do the 3-phase revision process.

Below is a handful of helpful hints to ensure that you avoid a negative experience:

Determine what is motivating someone to work with you. We all need to make a living, but if someone's sole reason for taking the job is financial I don't recommend hiring them. It is important that they have at least a passing interest in the topic of your book.

Take a serious look at the reviews and ratings of anyone who you are considering hiring.

Don't hire someone who is inexperienced, and try to confirm that their experience is relevant to your project.

Your voice is extremely important. Make sure that potential candidates understand what "voice" your book is written in, and that they are prepared to make edits with it in mind.

If there are doubts about agreement in any of these areas, do not move forward until you can come to a clear understanding. Then, get an agreement in writing before you begin the work. If you fail to come to an agreement DO NOT HIRE THEM!

The Three Week Time Limit

At Self-Publishing Pro we have set an obligatory 3 week time limit for the editing process. We find that this forced time constraint helps keep people focused – moving forward with a process which could otherwise drag on for months.

It is a rookie mistake to waste time and money unnecessarily on the editing process. To avoid this just follow what you've learned in the chapter. The 3 phase revision process, quick and easy editing, and how to find an amazing editor. By doing so you will breeze through this process saving you time, energy, and money.

It doesn't matter how many times you have to go back and forth with your editor – just make sure that they know you're serious about the three-week deadline. Your timeline should look something like this:

- Day 1: Hire your editor and set them up for success.
- Day 2-5: Editor completes first content edit.
- Day 6-8: You make changes to the first content edit.
- Day 9-12: Editor finalizes content edit and begins work on copy edit.
- Day 13-15: You approve changes and make final edits.
- Day 16-21: Editor completes a final copy edit and read through.

According to this schedule, you should only have to go back and forth a maximum of 3 times with your editor.

PRO TIP:

Monitor the work which is being done. You can track changes within both Google Docs and Microsoft Word, and "approve" or "deny" proposed edits. By doing so you will be able to witness the editing first hand.

Once you've finalize editing you'll be ready for the final stages before releasing your book! Getting your final draft back from the editor is a big accomplishment and deserves a moment of celebration.

In the next stage of this process you will learn the essential elements to formatting your book correctly and getting it ready for the big day. You're getting so close… Can you feel it?

CHAPTER 14

Format Your Book and Prepare for the Big Day

Formatting your book so that it is ready to be launched on Kindle can be confusing the first time around – but it doesn't have to be. I've laid the process out for you in an easy to understand way.

Kindle Formatting Simplified

Formatting your book will make you realize how close you actually are to finishing.

Below are your two options for formatting your book and registering it in the Kindle Store:

Hire a professional. This will cost you somewhere between $40 and $90, and I highly recommend it.

Do it yourself by modifying your Microsoft word file in a way that meets the kindle requirements. This is the route to go if money is really tight, or if you have an interest in learning the ins and outs of Kindle.

Amazon has instructions you can follow on http://kdp.amazon.com if this is something you want to spend your time doing.

Whichever route you decide to take, there are a few things which you need to check for before you or someone else begins working with your document:

- Make sure you have NO page numbers – page numbers vary according what device your book is being read on.
- NO text wrapping.
- NO use of bold or italics.

Outsourcing your Formatting Job

The process of finding someone to format your book is similar to that of finding an editor online, and I recommend heading to the Upwork site for this too.

All the same guidelines apply – make sure you are clear about your deadline and budget, and only consider those candidates who have formatting experience. Feel free to use the following template when posting your formatting job on the Upwork site.

Upwork Template for Book Formatter

> **Title**: I need a document converted to Mobi/Epub File for Kindle.
>
> **Body**: Please convert my (Word Doc/PDF) to an .Epub or .Mobi file.
>
> Convert file to be compatible for submission to Kindle.
>
> The (Word Doc/PDF) is (Insert # of pages).
>
> The deadline is tight and work must be completed by (insert date).
>
> Please DO NOT apply if you have never formatted for Kindle (through Kindle Direct Publishing).
>
> I will not hire a person who uses a converting software. I want this work to be done manually by a person who will go through the book and make sure that everything looks fine, that all the links are clickable and correct, and that there are no errors.
>
> If you can accomplish this job fulfilling all of the above requirements, please send me your proposal with the word "Juicy Mango" included at the top.

All you have to do is copy and paste your completed posting to the Upwork site, and choose your favorite candidate.

Preview Your Book

After your book is formatted, you will need to preview it to check for errors, and see how it looks on a Kindle device. For this purpose, you will be using the free software called "Kindle Previewer". Download it from this link, or find it through a Google search or the Kindle website.

In addition to showing you how your book will look on various devices such as Kindle E-reader, phone, or tablet, the Kindle Previewer allows you to check and make sure that all your links work.

After you fix any errors you find with the help of the Kindle Previewer, it's time to upload your book, sign up for a Kindle Direct Publishing (KDP) account, and create an Author Central profile.

Creating a KDP Account

If you're feeling excited, or perhaps a little nervous, as you're about to upload your book – that's great! This means that you're growing as a person.

Now it's time to create a KDP account in Amazon – which will allow you to track your sales, make technical and keyword changes, and change your price offers amongst other things.

To create this account, go to https://kdp.amazon.com and click on "Sign Up", or sign in using an existing Amazon account.

Then, follow the simple process of uploading and submitting your book, and…CONGRATULATIONS – you're now a published author!

PRO TIP:

You should only be publishing your book 3 – 5 days before your book launch. Only click "Save and Publish" if you're ready to publish. If not, click "Save as Draft", when you're finished uploading your book.

Creating an Author Central Profile

The vast majority of authors miss out on the benefits of creating an Author Central Profile, and the visibility within the Amazon Store which it ensures. However, after celebrating your success when you finally hit "Save and Publish", creating this profile should be your next step.

Having an Author Central profile will give you an edge over other authors who haven't bothered to create one. You can add a link to your book here, as well as an eye-catching book description. Adding a picture, a fun bio, and an optional video about yourself will let your readers get to know you a little better, and help them to connect to your work.

CHAPTER 15

Designing a Cover That Will Sell Your Book

Designing a cover for your book is tangible proof of all your hard work – making you feel amazing, as well as close to the finish line.

As a general rule, the best book covers are uncluttered, with images or designs which do not distract readers from the title. The books which stand out the most on Amazon have titles which are written in large, bold print. In the end, a bestselling cover is better than a great looking one.

You have 3 choices on how you can go about getting your cover completed:

- Choice 1: Create it yourself (free)
- Choice 2: Get it done for cheap
- Choice 3: Hire a professional designer

I highly recommend you get this done by a true professional (choice 3) because people really do judge a book its cover. For now I'll elaborate on your 3 choices.

Choice 1: Create it yourself (free)

Amazon has a built in cover creator that is a simple tool you can use to create the cover yourself. You can choose from multiple pre-made templates, change your color scheme, type in your title and subtitle and author name, click save and ta-da your book cover is done. This whole process only take a few minutes.

Choice 2: Get it done for cheap

One of the benefits of the times in which we are living in is that you can inexpensively outsource your cover design to someone who will appreciate the work. Instead of spending hours on Photoshop trying to do it yourself, you can hire an experienced designer for as little of $5.

Fiverr

My go-to outsourcing site is Fiverr (www.fiverr.com), where you can get many things done for a flat $5 fee. Just be aware that those $5 charges can add up fast, and you can end up spending more money than you planned – especially if you're not precise with your instructions.

If you want to use the services available on Fiverr to get your cover designed, head to the website and click on "find services" for "book cover", and browse through your choice of designers. I recommend that you sort by "High Rating", and only select a designer with a top rating, as well as lots of reviews and experience.

Once you find a few top-rated designers, buy multiple "gigs" totaling somewhere around $20 – then, click "order now", and checkout with PayPal. Simple as that.

The process of joining Fiverr is quick and easy. On the checkout page designers will ask you for some basic information, and you can share a brief design vision with them. For five bucks you won't be getting something high-end, but you'll end up with a cover which is good enough to start generating sales – and you can always re-design later.

Choice 3: Hire a professional designer

99 Designs

There are many other design platforms other than Fiver available, but they will be more expensive. Of these, 99 Designs is my favorite because on this site you can have over 30 designers working on your cover at the same time! Although this is pricier, I highly recommend you hire a true professional for this task.

If you design the cover yourself or hire a cheap designer people can tell just by looking at the quality workmanship and you don't want to leave a bad impression and miss out on the sale.

I know for myself if the cover looks like it was designed on Microsoft paint I won't buy the book. Even if it has a bunch of reviews and your buyers are most likely the same. Having a professional looking cover will also help you later on down the road if you plan on marketing your book to gain credibility and make yourself and authority.

Exactly how to design your cover professionally

If you go to www.99designs.com you will find a "How It Works" section which will walk you through the process of using this site, step by step. Essentially, you will create a "design brief" and submit it. Then, designers from all over the world start creating competing cover designs, and you get to choose the one you like the most.

Step 1: Be Extremely Specific

In your design brief you will explain exactly what you need, so try your best to express your precise needs.

By explaining upfront your ideal cover, your vision, the exact colors you want, this provides the designers with a foundation to work from.

Below is the design brief I used when soliciting a design cover for my first book. Feel free to use it to make your own.

Design Brief Example

> TITLE: (Insert Your Book Title)
>
> Author's Name: (Insert Your Name)
>
> The cover including the back and spine needs to be simple and bold – something which will pop in Amazon's Kindles store as a thumbnail, and on the bookshelf. The book measures 5.5 × 8.5, and the spine will be approximately .72.
>
> This book is about _____.
>
> It's very important the book "pop off the shelf", and catch the eye. I am open to any image or illustration you choose. The most important thing for us is that the cover sells, not

just that it looks pretty. It should be polished, engaging, and interesting.

I like a bold color palette and a cover that lets the reader know right away what the book is about. Nothing too busy, and a simple color scheme with only 2 or 3 colors.

Example or books whose covers I like are:

(Do your research, then provide a list of 5 books)

Step 2: Ask for multiple formats

Its very important that you ask the winning cover designer upfront for multiple formats. You will need these later for your eBook on kindle and for marketing purposes on other platforms.

First request for a 3D image of the book so you can use that for marketing, then request for a 3D image of the book with a Cd image next to the book. Second ask for a generic format so you can use this later after your KDP select agreement expires. You will use this format for Nook and iBooks (if you choose to go this route).

By asking up front they won't charge you later, because it's very little effort on their part to make your cover into different formats.

Step 3: Get your cover created at a width of 90 pixels

When browsers are shopping on the Amazon marketplace they will see your book cover thumbnail in the size of 90 pixels.

So make sure your title and subtitle is readable when the designer resized your cover down to 90 pixels in width.

Added bonus of using 99 designs

You also get to rate all the work generated for you, by giving designers anywhere from one to five stars. In addition, you can leave comments on designs, allowing designers to make changes based on your feedback. Keep refining the designs until you choose 2 or 3 that you really like.

You will take these few designs and use 99 designs cool social media rating feature that their system has built into it. This allows you to select your top favorite designs and share them on social media, allowing your friends and followers to vote on which one they like best. This allows for valuable feedback, while also generating some buzz about your upcoming book by allowing people to feel involved in the process.

Once you select a winning cover, the designer will send you high quality files as well as the copyright, and you're good to go!

PRO TIP:

Get your cover design started and finished quickly. Give yourself a deadline of 2 weeks – you can always have the designer edit it later. **Remember: DONE IS BETTER THAN PERFECT.**

By following the guidance in this chapter you will get your cover designed fast and efficiently. Most importantly you will feel rejuvenated with how close you are to finishing this dream of yours.

As a reminder you can design the cover by yourself, hire someone on Fiverr, or get 30+ professionals to compete for your work on 99 designs.

In the next chapter you will learn how to leverage social media and generate a buzz about your book. This little trick that you're about to learn will make people line up to buy your book.

CHAPTER 16

Generating Excitement About Your Book

After successfully uploading your book, increasing your visibility by creating an Author Central account, and finishing your cover design it's time to start marketing your book even before its release.

I'm going to show you a number of ways that you can generate excitement about your book before launching it, without turning people off through shameful self-promotion on social media.

7 Ninja Marketing Hacks

It's very important to get people anticipating your book in the weeks prior to its release. You need to create excited fans!

One of the easiest ways of doing this is through your social media platforms. The people who you love and trust, will always be there to support your efforts – but you need to reach others as well.

When I wrote my first book I had zero audience, and maybe you find yourself in the same boat. However, being an unknown author does not have to hinder your success.

Even if you are an established author, I'll show you how to leverage social media and text messaging to boost your launch week – getting you a boatload of sales and downloads.

When I released ***Visions to the Top***, I decided to upload three possible cover designs on Facebook and asked people to weigh in on their favorite. This caused my newsfeed to BLOW UP! People love to give you their feedback – so take advantage of this strategy to promote your book.

Getting people involved in the process of publishing your book by asking for their input helps to establish an emotional connection with them. This will help them not only care about you, but also about the success of your book.

Letting people vote on a cover design gets them involved early, and they are sure to be interested in knowing which design won.

When launch day comes, these same people will be ready to jump when you ask them to; and some of them may already have opted into your pre-launch funnel.

Here is one template of the 7 ninja marketing hacks we used on Facebook to help promote ***Visions to the Top***. This stuff really does work and social media users excited to participate.

Cover Competition (Post 2 – 3 weeks before your launch)

> Hey Friends!
>
> I need a little help from you. I'm narrowing down my top choices for the front cover design of my new book.
>
> I've picked my top 3 favorites, and instead of choosing the finalist myself I'd like it if you could take a few seconds to let me know your favorite.
>
> So… please vote by "liking" your favorite cover design.
>
> Feel free to comment with any feedback.
>
> Thanks so much for your help!

By keeping your audience updated about the results of the cover competition, you will be keeping your book in the forefront of their minds – building excitement around its release.

Create Posts for Other Milestones to Generate Even More Anticipation.

You can also create posts for other milestones in your publishing process, such as:

- Sharing the results of the cover competition
- Announcement the pre-release date – "My book (insert title) will be free on (insert date).

- Announce your Launch date.

- Launch Week Celebration: "Thanks for all your help, we finally made it!"

- Bestseller status update: "We're now ranked #1 in____categories.

- Announcement of Audio Book release

- Announcement of Paperback cover release.

PRO TIP #1:

Resist the urge to respond to people's posts immediately. Wait until between 6 and 9 pm – these are prime hours which will boost your post back to the top of the news feed.

PRO TIP #2

Copy and paste your post to any groups which you are a member of on Facebook, making sure to respond in the same way I suggested in the previous tip.

Book Marketing To Dos

Most people have no idea how to market or launch their first book. Fortunately, it's my strength, and I'll be sharing everything you need to know about launching your first book and marketing it.

When you're ready to launch your book, I recommend that you use my easy to follow checklist as a guide. This comprehensive marketing checklist can be found at https://self-publishingpro.com/blf-free-resources

Schedule a Launch Date

Once you're editing and formatting is complete, you need to schedule a launch date for your book.

We often get asked what a reasonable timeline for the launching of a book should be. Generally speaking, your launch should take place no more than 2 to 3 weeks after your editing and formatting has been finalized.

As with the editing process, we recommend that you don't drag your feet – prolonging your launch unnecessarily. Just set a date, and stick to it. Better yet – announce this date on social media so that you will be held accountable to it.

Clicking "Publish" might seem like a frightening prospect, but believe me – it is an exciting feeling which creates such a sense of accomplishment.

By using the 7 ninja marketing hacks on social media, the book marketing to do's, and scheduling your launch date you will be ready to launch your book with a bang.

In the next chapter you will learn critical techniques for launching your book and how the pros do it, which will guarantee your book blast off from the start.

CHAPTER 17

Launching Your Book The Pro Way

The weeks before the launching of your book are critical to its success. The following are important suggestions for things you can do to make the most of this time. I personally used these strategies myself and they work like a charm

Building Your List for Success

After drumming up interest on social media and establishing a launch date, it's time to start building a pre-release list. This consists of the emails of anyone and everyone who has demonstrated an interest in buying your book before, or when it is released.

Learning to create and use a pre-release list is the best way to build an audience of people who are generally interested in your book. Anyone who has been part of your social media marketing campaign will fall into this category - they are already invested in your success.

Everyone on your pre-release list should receive emails during launch week, which will provide updates as you approach your release date. The idea is to get as many people as possible to download your book and leave a review.

Your main goal is to get people involved early so when you do go live on Amazon they promote your book for you. You do this by releasing the book for free with the goal of getting thousands of downloads. Then you will slowly increase your price over the following weeks. This creates urgency and people will buy it before the price goes up. We will talk more about this in a bit.

When I launched *Visions to the Top* I only had 79 people on my pre-release list, but guess what? All 79 of them were interested in buying and reviewing my book!

These 79 downloads and reviews helped my book to rank as a bestseller – giving it the traction and momentum it needed to drive sales, which continue to roll into this day.

Doing an effective pre-launch is a vast topic that we could spend hours on, however Its best to keep things simple so I'll you a 7 step roadmap to guide you through what should be done and when, because your first book launch can be a bit overwhelming.

Don't despair – this easy, step-by-step method for launching your book which I'm going to outline for you is foolproof. It is the same one I use for launching my books, and it has been used time and again by authors across the globe, as well as Self Publishing Pro members

Allow yourself to learn from my mistakes – I've analyzed what works, tested it myself, and ironed out the glitches. The task is the very simple, but is loaded with an effective strategy I'm going to provide you with.

That said, you will have the flexibility to make some adjustments to this plan, deciding what you think will work best for your particular book. Follow this guideline, and enjoy a successful launch:

Step 1: Pre-Launch

A few weeks before the publication date you're going to want to reach out to podcasters, bloggers, and journalists for Forbes.com and Huffington Post. I'll teach you how to do this in chapter 20. This strategy will open the door for you so you can let influencers know that you have a book that's about to be released on "insert your topic".

Most importantly they want to know how it will benefit them or their audience. So tell them that you are going to provide a guest post article or can do a live interview if they are interested.

Have your early readers aka your close friends and family read through your book and prepare an honest testimonial so when your book does go live they will be able to upload their review immediately.

PRO TIP: Reviews are absolutely crucial for your success because Amazon sees these as a signal of a book that is quality. So it's very important that you get honest and authentic reviews because Amazon can possibly detect if they are fake or bought. There would be nothing worse than to write a great book and it be taken down from fraudulent reviews.

Another great resource I provide all my Self-Publishing Pro clients with is the many Facebook groups and book forums where there are literally hundreds of thousands of book junkies, I mean readers who love downloading and buying books when they are free and before the price is risen to $2.99.

You can find these sites through research by looking for online pages that accept submissions for free Kindle books. Keep in mind you must submit your application to these submission sites sometimes weeks before the day you need them.

Step 2: Upload Your Book

When you go to upload your book MAKE SURE you do it three to five days before your launch.

Pro Tip: Use the Kindle Previewer one week before your three to five day free promo launch to make sure it's formatted properly (in MOBI or ePUB file) Doing so will ensure you peace of mind that everything looks proper for the big day.

Always remember that you have the option of enlisting help from freelancers on Upwork.com if you feel you need a little help.

Step 3: Inflate The Price During The Free Promo

You will get the option of including a price at which it will cost after the free promotion is over. I recommend you take advantage of this moment and set your books price to an inflated $4.99-$9.99.

During your free promo Kindle does a fantastic job marketing your book and showing its readers that they should get it while it's free. They will strike-through the future cost and show the savings amount. To see an example of what it will look like look at the image below.

The readers will notice it's free and will see it's normally cost (whatever you set the cost to be). I don't recommend you going over $9.99 because books on kindle normally don't cost that much.

This little trick helps big time to boost downloads, get "Amazon Juice", and will increase your sales once you change your book from free to paid (which you will learn in step 5).

Digital List Price: $9.99 What's this? ☑
Kindle Price: $0.00
You Save: $9.99 (100%)

Step 4: The 5 Day Free Book Launch

Amazon will let you publish your book for free for the first five days if you enroll through their KDP select program. I recommend you start your promo on Sunday. This will allow you to get downloads and reviews from readers before the week gets into full swing. It also gives you a jump on other authors who opt to release their book on Tuesdays.

You'll be climbing the charts when others are just launching their book, and your free promo will end on Thursday – before the down days of Friday and Saturday.

This is the approach I recommend you follow because your main objective is to get a bunch of downloads.

On top of this I recommend you do the 5 day free launch because gives you a little wiggle room as well as the chance to modify it slightly to suit your book

The other option you have is doing a 2-3 day free promotion but that may leave you with less room for error. This approach does stirs up a sense of urgency in readers who want to get it for free. Again if you're a first time author I recommend you stick with the free 5 day promo.

Consider advertising in advance on social media and through text messages – making people feel the need to jump on the bandwagon while your book is still free. You can say something like:

> Hey Friends – I have decided to offer my book for FREE for one more day to let any stragglers take advantage of this offer. Get it FREE in the next 24 hours! (Insert Link)"

PRO TIP: The choice of free promo is ultimately your decision, but whichever you choose – advertise that it will ONLY last 2-3 days.

This way, if your book is doing well you have the option to cancel the promo and start charging after 2 or 3 days. Alternatively, if you need a few more days to help your book climb the charts – it can be extended to five days.

Also, make sure to schedule your promo in KDP a minimum of 24 hours before you want it to start, and shorten your URL by going to https://goo.gl/ to make it easier on viewer's eyes.

(Optional) Text every contact in your phone saying:

> Hey (Insert Their Name)
>
> I have decide to give my book away for free a limited time! Can you download it, read through it and leave a review? We are so close to hitting #1 and breaking a record!
>
> Again it'll only be free during this stage.
>
> Here is the link, if you can please help by downloading and leaving a review on Amazon (Insert Shortened link)
>
> Thanks for your help!

You will be blown away how many people will do what you ask!

Yes you won't make money initially from this approach but it will help you gain traction, get "Amazon juice" and move your book towards the top ranks which will ultimately be better for you in the long run.

Step 5: Offer Your Book for $0.99 for One Week

After your free promo is over, keep your book price at $0.99 for one week. This strategy is designed to give your book time to climb the paid charts.

During this week, focus on gathering as may reviews as possible, and continue to drive sales to your book. Text or email all your contacts providing them with your shortened URL, promote yourself on a podcast, have your social media friends share your post – whatever it takes!

(Optional) Send this text message to all your contacts:

> Thanks for being a part of my book launch & if you downloaded the book while it was free that helped. If you could please buy it at $.99 before the price goes up.
>
> I'd appreciate if you bought it because it will help with the Amazon algorithm massively! A purchase weighs much heavier & helps us towards our goal of reaching the TOP #1 spot (insert tiny URL link)

You'll be surprised how many people will buy your book at $.99 just to help you out. Getting sales is important because these weighs more than the free downloads. Amazon will promote your book to all its customer if they notice you are making sales. SO PUSH HARD!

You should also promote your book on the book submission pages I referenced in the last section. "Only $.99 for (insert number of days)"

Step 6: Slowly Nudge Your Price Up

After a week at $0.99, slowly nudge your book price up to either $1.99 or $2.99. Then, increase your price to 2.99 seven days later.

Each time you increase your book price, consider writing a message at the top of your book description as follows:

"For the next five days of our launch, we have discounted our price. Be sure to get a copy now, before the price jumps back up to $2.99 on Friday (04/20)."

If you opt to add a note like this to your book description, make sure to include a date to encourage people to take immediate action.

Also, only do this if you actually intend to increase the price. Operating with integrity is of the utmost importance when you're trying to build a following.

Step 7: Re-launch Your Book Through Promotions

Inside KDP select, every 90 days you have the option to offer your book for free for 5 days like you just learned. This is helpful because it will keep your book on the top of the charts and allow you to get reviews.

KDP select also allow you to run a "Kindle Countdown Deal" which is helpful because Amazon will put a countdown timer next to your book and show it discounted so their buyers can buy it at a great price.

I recommend you run these promotions to keep your buzz going years after its first release. By following these 7 steps you will launch your book the pro way.

CHAPTER 18

Tips On How To Become A Best Selling Author

Becoming a best-selling author is awesome! It's not the most difficult thing to do but at the same time it's not the easiest task.

Everybody always ask me what does it mean to become an Amazon best-selling author, and basically what this means is that you rank at the #1 spot in a specific category within Amazon.

If you follow the 7 steps I've just outlined, it is very likely that you will make it as an Amazon best seller into the "Hot New Releases" section on Amazon!

Hot New Releases include all the best-selling books of the last 30 days. The 3 top Hot New Releases will actually appear in a sidebar which people will see as they are browsing the bestseller list.

Making it to the top three in the Hot New Releases will help you to dramatically expand your audience, and getting to the top 3 in any category is where the real money is. Book sales generally break down as follows:

- Top 3 Books – represent 50 – 60% of all book purchases
- Top 7 – 10 Books – represent 30 – 40% of all book purchases
- All Other Books: split the rest of sales (which are rare and occasional)

So staying up top will ultimately result in more sales. Being on the Hot New Releases list for as long as possible is hugely important – this is why you need to upload your book 3 to 5 days before your actual launch.

Kindle has updated its rules so that now your clock starts running the moment you hit publish.

The photo below illustrates the power of leverage created by the Hot New Releases list. During the launch of *Visions to the Top* I took this screenshot, and added some cool graphics using www.canva.com. I was then able to use it for marketing my book on social media. Once the book hit #1 on the Hot New Releases sidebar, it immediately skyrocketed to #1 in multiple categories.

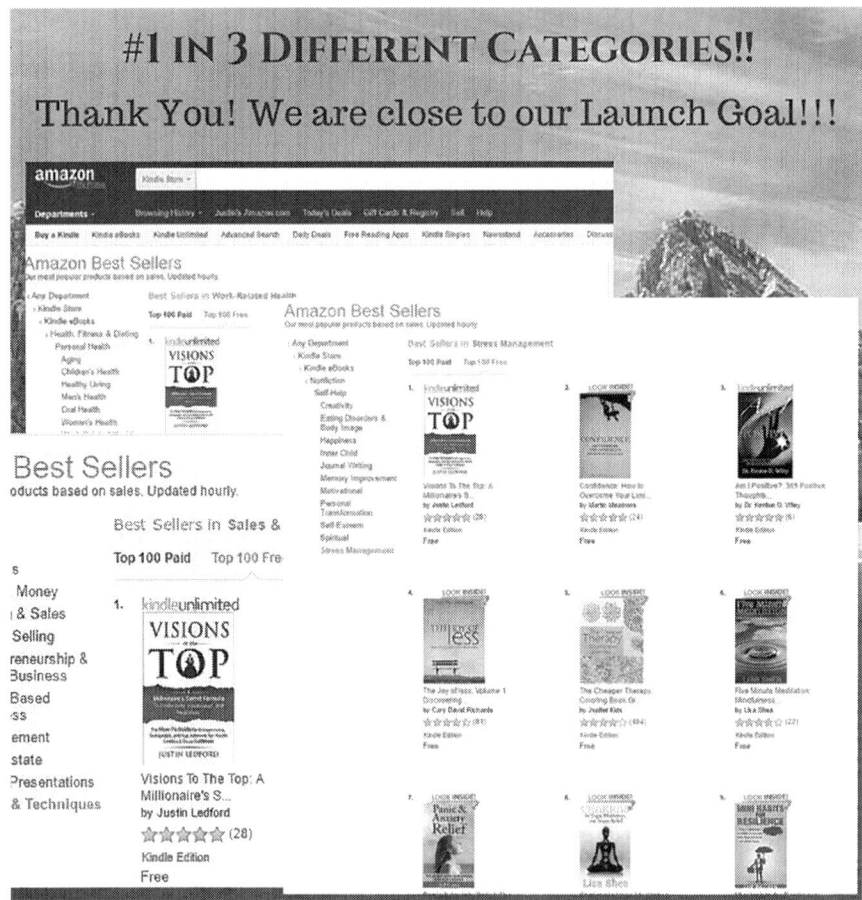

I felt incredibly grateful to be able to take this image, and my family and friends were so proud. It was awesome! My book made it to the #1 spot in 3 categories, and was ahead of Napoleon Hill's legendary book "Think and Grow Rich".

My hope is that you have the opportunity to have the same feelings of gratitude, happiness and joy that I experienced.

By becoming a #1 best-selling author on Amazon you have a lot credibility when you speak to people. They will immediately listen to whatever you say, and people will see you as the expert. There are a few things you must do to make this a reality.

1) Choosing the Right Categories is Crucial

You should aim high at whatever you do in life and your goal should be to become an Amazon best-selling author. In this section I will teach you the key elements you must do to make it to the #1 spot in a specific category within Amazon.

First choose to place your book in a low competition category and plan on telling everyone you know to buy your book while it's $.99 as well as post it on the online forums while your book is such a low cost.

The key is to find these low competition categories. You can find them by looking for the #1 best-selling book that has an Amazon Best Sellers Rank of 4,000 - 50,000. I recommend stay around the 20,000 range.

To find the Amazon Best Sellers Rank click on the #1 book and scroll down and you will see its rank like the photo below.

This rank indicates how well it's selling on Amazon. So the larger the rank number is, the fewer amount of books being sold. For example a booked ranked at 22,000 is selling fewer copies than a book ranked at 1,500.

Amazon doesn't really publish data on exact figures but many authors have posted their results online and through research I have found that with an Amazon Bestseller Ranking of 900 is selling around 100 copies a day, 20,000 is selling around 15 copies a day, 50,000 is selling around four to five copies a day.

Ultimately if your goal is to make an impact and make money what you need to do is find the #1 best-selling book that has a rank of around 20,000 and jot that category down. If it makes sense to put your book there you will make nice passive income each month from your book.

2) Put Your Book In the Right Category

So if you goal is make money, make an impact, and use your book to open doors in your life, then it's important that you follow this section because becoming an Amazon bestseller will do just that.

You should also learn how to categorize your book so that it will rank highly in any given niche. A strategy we recommend is cross-categorization. This involves selecting two different main categories and then sub-categories for these (for example: "Health, Fitness & Dieting", AND "Self-help", rather than picking 2 subcategories under one main category).

If you make the mistake of selecting two subcategories under the same main category, you will only be reaching half as many people. Remember to take a look at the bestsellers in the category which matches your book best, then select subcategories which will help your book rank at the top of this niche.

Select categories which you know that you can rank high in – ones which aren't very competitive will help keep you from getting lost in the sea of books sold on Amazon.

PRO TIP:

When deciding on subcategories, look for signs that they are ones that you can rank high in. For example, if you see that the number one book in a subcategory is 4,000 or higher in its ranking, this is a sure sign that you book should be there!

All the information which you need to know about rankings is available to you under "product details" when you click on the top selling books in your prospective categories.

Here is a prime example of how to look for good categories to choose:

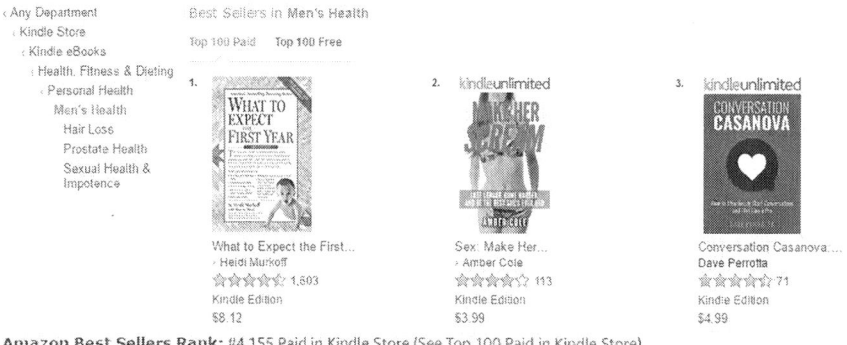

You will notice the number one book in this sub-category has an overall ranking of 4,610 in the Paid Kindle Store. If your book was relevant to this genre you can be sure that "Health, Fitness, & Dieting", and "Nonfiction are great categories for you – because this book has a ranking of over 4,000.

Again just to recap find two low competition categories to put your book under and you will have twice the amount of chances to be a success and become an #1 Amazon Best Selling Author.

If for whatever reason you list your book and it doesn't end up in the right category, then contact the support team and politely ask them to publish your book in the right categories. Below is the message you can send.

> Hello,
>
> Can you please put my book (Insert Your Book Title) in the following two categories because they are not where I originally expected them to be?
>
> Category 1: Kindle Store > Kindle eBooks > Nonfiction > Self-Help > Inner Child
>
> Category 2: Kindle Store > Kindle eBooks > Religion &

Spirituality > New Age > Meditation

Thank you so much!

Keep in mind it might take a day or two for them to respond, but they are generally really good about responding and will change it for you.

Tip 3) Generate over 16 sales

To make it best seller status all you have to do is focus on making sales right when your book becomes $.99. Some people say all you need to sell is 5 copies while others say it takes over 20 copies sold on day 1. I always recommend you aim for a minimum of 15 sales on the first day. So right when you launch make sure you tell all your friends and family to purchase your book when it turns to $.99

People will be glad to help you hit your goal of being a number bestselling author on Amazon. Shoot for more than 15 sales though. I recommend you shoot for 25-30 sales. Once you hit best seller status immediately capture that image and share it with everyone you care about. You will feel more proud that day than almost any other accomplishment in your life!

Amazon will tag your book with an orange banner that says "#1 Best Seller". Enjoy this moment, screenshot it, blast it out to the world. By being an Amazon bestseller you immediately gain instant credibility.

That success will generate sales for a long time, not only in book royalties but in the doors that open for you in your life.

In summary choosing the right categories and focusing on generating sales from the get go will pay off big time and allow you to become an Amazon Best Seller.

Once you hit this status new doors will open for you and in the next chapter you will be reminded of just how much writing your book can impact your life before we move on to my favorite section which is marketing.

CHAPTER 19

Writing a Book Will Transform Your Life

By now I hope that you can see that although there are a number of steps involved in writing and publishing a book, it is a simple process which is well within your reach.

You've learned how to come up with a book idea from scratch, how to create a Mind Map and generate an outline from it.

We showed you how to find and work with an editor to turn your writing into a masterpiece.

You also learned how to create a title that will sell your book, as well as where and how to get your cover designed. Finally, we taught you how to position your book as a money making machine, by using Amazon algorithms.

You now know everything you need to know in order to write that bestselling book which will begin to earn you authority, as well as a passive income.

The good news is - it doesn't end there! Writing your first book will change your life in so many positive ways. Becoming a published author will open many doors for you – both money and new opportunities will start to show up monthly.

I have had the good fortune to be able to witness the success of many clients as they go from first time writers to bestselling authors in a variety of genres. I have witnessed the transformation which occurs as people go on to live the life of their dreams – all as the result of writing a book or two.

Writing a book opens the door to so many spontaneous adventures!

A great example is my personal friend Hal Elrod who wrote ***The Miracle Morning: The Not-So-Obvious Secret Guaranteed to***

Transform Your Life (Before 8 AM). Writing this book not only helped him increase his bank balance tenfold, but helped him create the type of life most people only dream of.

Hal's book opened doors for him across the globe. He has spoken as a keynote speaker at numerous international events, making as much as $10,000 per engagement. He is now a coach and mentor to some of the most successful people in the world, his life will never be the same again.

Writing a book has the power to transform your life too. Next, I will go into some of the ways in which this is possible.

The Benefits of Writing a Book

The benefits of writing a book are many – some of which I've already mentioned. As we near the end of this book, I'd like to summarize, once again, exactly what they are, using examples from the many people who I've seen achieve amazing results from their new status as author.

Hopefully, this will drive home the fact that once it is completed and published, your book will take on a very powerful life of its own. Seven of the amazing benefits of writing a bestselling book are as follows:

The Ability to Create a Passive Source of Income

The number one reason why most people entertain the idea of writing a book, is for its potential to create a passive source of income. I know that I am grateful for the monthly income which I receive through Amazon for my book sales!

A personal friend of mine name Steve Scott consistently makes from 30k-60k a month from the books he's written. Over the course of several years he has written multiple books that passively pay him better than what most people make in a whole year. The only difference between him and you is he got started earlier.

Authors who have self-published their books on Amazon now make more money than those who have books published by one of the five major publishing houses. Self-publishing is clearly the way of the future.

Although you are able to make some serious income as a published author, this is only one of the many ways in which Self-Publishing Pro students have used their bestselling books to create the life of their dreams.

Expanding Your Reach

Many people have discovered that writing a book is an excellent way to generate leads for their business. In our own experience, publishing our books has resulted in 8-10 leads a day, and has helped us to build a contact list of 4,500 in a very short time.

This in turn results in more business income, as leads get converted into paying clients. If you want to start a new business, or grow your current one – don't underestimate the power of your book as a way of expanding your reach.

Increasing Coaching and Speaking Opportunities

Before I published ***Visions to the Top,*** my speaking and coaching opportunities were limited, but since I became a published author I am consistently receiving paid opportunities to do both.

Even if you are a seasoned coach or motivational speaker, having a bestselling book is an amazing way to increase your opportunities – as well as your fees!

A book will help you establish your authority, and being seen as an expert in your field will allow you to powerfully impact your industry.

Many graduates of Self-Publishing Pro have gone on to grow their businesses, and impact others with coaching and speaking opportunities.

Shortly after finishing The Power to Change Eric Gillman has been able to fulfill his lifelong dream of becoming a paid speaker at multiple events across the country!

Free Marketing Through Added Exposure

Having a published book increases your opportunity to appear on TV, radio, podcasts, and on major Internet sites such as The Huffington Post.

Many authors of our program have benefited from their books in these ways, if you have a limited marketing budget you should be aware that the amount of FREE publicity you'll get as the result of your bestselling book is truly amazing.

Building Your Business

Whether you're building a business from the ground up, or trying to expand one you currently own – writing a book can single handedly help you more than anything else.

Although a book is not a business, it can help you generate opportunities which can either become a business, or help you grow an existing one.

I've had the privilege of watching people use their books to help them sell services and products in a wide variety of industries, including health and nutrition, coaching and financial services.

The truth is, no matter what your line of work, a book can help you boost your business.

Getting Your Foot in the Door

Many people now consider a bestselling book to be the greatest calling card – your invitation through an important door to land a big deal or make an amazing new contact.

Instead of handing contacts your business card, imagine being able to hand them a signed copy of your latest bestseller! Rather than losing it or throwing it away, it will more than likely find a place on a shelf in their office – where they will think about you every time they see it.

If you want to focus on expanding your business network, consider the fact that a published book will provide you with the respect and authority you need in order to do so.

Doing Business Locally

Owning and operating a local business comes with its own set of challenges – demanding a level of trust not necessary if you're dealing with people who are relatively unknown to you.

Your prospects are more likely to trust you and value your expertise if you have published a book about your line of work. So whether you're a plumber, landscaper, lawyer, or financial consultant – being a bestselling author can help you sell yourself and your local business!

These 7 benefits will allow multiple opportunities to arrive into your life. Most importantly you will feel proud of yourself… That is a feeling that is worth its weight in gold.

CHAPTER 20

Market Your Book Like A Business

Now if you really want to make money, I'm talking long term passive income then I recommend you market your book just like you would market a business. You can write a great book, with specific keywords, in a niche category and make good money off of it just sitting back and letting Amazon do all the work for you.

But if you want guaranteed long term financial success from your book then you're going to need to market it.

If you've never been in business for yourself, the word marketing sounds scary. No worries though because my profession has been marketing and sales for over a decade now. This is the stuff that really lights me up.

Marketing is a contest for people's attention and like Steve Jobs said a lot of times, people don't know what they want until you show it to them. So what I like to recommend all my clients at Self-Publishing Pro who want to really build a nice passive income from one single book is to market their book by using these strategies.

1) Get interviewed on podcasts

There are thousands of podcasts (Internet radio shows) available today and each host has their own community or audience that listens to them. Each host is hungry for new content and wants to interview interesting people. Podcast are GOLD MINES for an author.

My friend Hal Elrod told me if you get booked on 100-300 podcasts, share a compelling well-crafted story, make your message specifically tailored to their audience, and have a call to action at the end that message, you can retire rich from what will happen to your book's success!

In fact here is what he said about podcasts being a great tool to sell books:

"Having just surpassed 100,000 copies sold (and with over 1,000+ 5 star reviews) for my self-published book, ***The Miracle Morning: The Not-So-Obvious Secret Guaranteed to Transform Your Life***, I can confidently say that the number one key to driving book sales has been securing interviews on other people's podcasts!

It used to be TV shows that you wanted to get on to sell books. However, not only are the podcasts now proving to sell more books than TV, they're free to get booked on! I've invested over $10,000 to get myself booked on 15 local and national TV shows (and saw very little increase in sales) and then invested zero dollars to get booked on over 200 podcasts, which has driven my sales to as 10,900+ copies in a month."

Even if you prefer to be introverted like myself, just inform the host and they will guide you by asking all the questions, and after you do it a couple times you will gain confidence. Because the best way to gain confidence is to do what you are afraid to do.

When you release your book to the world you will want to practice with up and coming podcaster and you can find these on i-tune by searching inside the new-and-noteworthy section. These podcasters are up and comers and are gaining momentum in the Internet radio world.

There are 3 steps to getting booked on these new and noteworthy shows.

1. Select the category you want to approach (by clicking on the all categories drop down menu).

2. Listen to an episode, leave a 5 star review with a positive comment

3. Send them a series of emails. Here is the first email that works well, but sometimes you have to send them multiple emails:

    Dear (insert name)

I respect your time at the highest level, and wanted to appreciate you in advance for reading this! I first wanted to thank you for all that you do for people, and see if there is anything I could do to add value, promote, or spread the word about your podcast to my circle of influence. I've been following you for quite some now. (I am a Bestselling author of ***Visions to the Top***) and really love what you've done, and 100% believe in your cause, structure, and the legacy your building.

Is there anything specific you're doing now that you're trying to promote or something I can share?

I'm a big fan of your podcast. I particularly liked your episode (The Ways to maximize energy when you were talking about, how to maximize your energy without drinking caffeine or taking other stimulants. I also enjoyed learning that taking more breaks at work will actually increase your productivity, and the amount of exercise you need daily to increase your ability to focus, be creative, make decisions and to stay alert). I know that being a leader can be a thankless job, so please know your work is making a difference in people's lives. It has mine.

Anyway, since we're both in the business of (writing and speaking). I thought I'd share your message with my audience, even if it not as large as yours. (I have been pushing my limits for years now by pursuing extreme sports like free diving, and backcountry snowboarding, and travel all over the world to follow these passions. I help people learn how to activate their inner power by using visualization, meditation, and productivity hacks that have allow me to build million dollar businesses). So I think we have a nice alignment in how we serve. I've subscribed to your podcast and left a 5 star review as well and shared with my sales team

Thanks once again for all you do, it is truly appreciated. Please let me know what you'd like me to tell my audience about and how I can help you. Looking forward to hearing from you!

Much Respect

Justin Ledford

Let's Connect!

Everything in the parenthesis is what you would change. This approach works really well with new and noteworthy podcasters and once you get on several shows use those as leverage to approach the big dogs with hundreds of thousands and even millions of listeners.

This is how you get yourself in front of your unique audience by leveraging the podcasters audience. By using this approach you can reach literally millions of people. Hence do this 100-300 times and your will laughing your way to the bank every month.

2) Get featured on Forbes, Huffington Post, INC, Elite Daily, Etc.

Getting featured on these big name websites will boost your book sales like crazy, increase your authority, and make you feel super cool :) The approach is pretty straightforward and consist of 3 steps

1. Go to these popular websites where your ideal customers hang out. For example if your book is about success principles, you'd go to Forbes.com or Huffington Post. Next in the search bar type in a keyword that is related to your book topic. Then several articles will pull up, from there click on the article and find out who the contributor was (who wrote it)

2. Use the same email above and once they respond tell them you'd like to write a short and concise press release for them to share.

3. Watch your book sales SOAR!

My article was shared over 17,000 times on these websites!

Remember these people you are contacting want new content. So your mentality should be that you are doing them a favor and not the other way around. You don't want to come off as needy.

This step is like planting seeds… Not every seed you sow will reap a fruit, but the ones that do will give you your bounty. It helps to have multiple emails prepared for these contributors and podcasters and once you start gaining momentum by being interviewed on different shows/press release then in your follow up emails mention what shows you have been on.

There are many forms of marketing you can do. I just mention these because you can do these on your spare time around your busy life. If your book truly is a passion project then it should be fun to market it, so I recommend you write on a topic that you care about because there is a high chance you will get the opportunity to talk about your book for years and years to come.

Marketing on the web is powerful because you never know how far and wide your reach will go. These strategies work as long as you're willing to put forth the effort. Fortune favors the bold so be bold in your pursuit 100 podcast/blog post and beyond and you'll be able to enjoy the life most only dream of.

PRO TIP: If you plan on marketing your book then it is a must that you format your book into an audiobook and paperback copy. Just doing this will allow you to make 3 times the income. Some people will prefer to read it straight off their kindle device, while others rather listen to it, and of course you have the folks who like a good old fashioned book in their hands

Change The Way You See Yourself

Apart from any external changes you may experience, writing a book can completely change the way you see yourself.

Jenna Bayne, one of our clients, has been a life strategist for teens with eating disorders for over 7 years now. Her passion is helping teens to realize how special they are while helping them overcome their bad had eating habits. Through the process she witnesses transformation of these individuals and helps them to believe they can be anything they want to be…

But buried deep inside she was saddened because she had a faded dream of being a published author.

Shortly after joining Self-Publishing Pro she became a woman on a mission and within 90 days completed her first children's book.

I am Part of Nature went on to become a bestseller and has moved so many families' hearts. She is now more inspired than ever before because of her level of contribution and greater impact she can provide to the youth of the world.

This single book has lit a fire within her, and given her an increased appreciation with the career path she has been guided to pursue. She has never been more confident in her abilities and enjoys the many benefits of being a published author

Jessie Wright is a female entrepreneur who always had the dream of writing a book that would inspire women by helping them transform their life to become their own boss. She told me her goal was to become a best-selling author to build a passive income, open new doors, and become a dominate figure in the personal growth community. She told me she wanted to finish her book around her full time business, and she did!

She is a great example to her family and friends that you really can accomplish anything you set your mind to do. Her book makes her stand out in crowds and networking and she says it helps because now people listen to her with a different intrigue and intensity.

Can you imagine yourself as a bestselling author – commanding greater respect, a higher salary, and creating a legacy for yourself?

A bestselling book will help you gain financial and personal freedom, while impacting your business in a way which nothing else can.

Believe me when I tell you that a bestselling book can be the foundation upon which you can build not only a passive income, and increased business opportunities – but also self-respect, and influence.

CHAPTER 21

It's Time To Get In The Game!

Now that you've finished reading this book, you know everything necessary to write and publish your own bestseller.

Follow the plan as I've outlined it, and I can promise you success. The process is simple, and easy – and designed to help you avoid the many rookie mistakes I made with my first book.

The guidelines I've laid down are foolproof, and have helped many people across the globe become bestselling authors.

All that remains is for you to take the next step, and get into the game!

If someone like me who disliked writing and wasn't very good at it can become a bestselling author, so can you!

The key to your success lies in taking consistent action, staying focused on your goal, having accountability, and taking one step at a time. – Make the decision that you will write your book and be victorious!

If Brianna Greenspan, a sales lady, can self-publish her first book in 3 months, then so can you.

If Matt Duncan, a sustainability consultant, can become a best-selling author, then you can to.

If Jenna Bayne, a life strategist for teens can follow her passion and write a best-selling children's book, then so can you.

If Jessie Wright, an entrepreneur, can write a book that inspires women across the globe, while running a full time business, then so can you.

If Eric Gillman, a "man with no extra time" can write a book that gets him speaking and coaching engagements, then so can you.

You will have to make some sacrifices in the process of writing your book. You may lose some sleep to early mornings or late nights. You might have to forgo some nights out with friends and family, or some episodes of your favorite TV show. Just know that the benefits of a bestselling book will far outweigh any of the things you give up.

Sharing my success strategies with you that I figured out the hard serves my higher purpose in life. My desire is to reach out and help as many people as possible to build the life of their dreams, and a leave a legacy for their family and friends.

I established Self-Publishing Pro in order to help people change their lives – through the process of writing and publishing their own books.

Reading this book is evidence of the fact that you have a story you'd like to share with the world – for whatever reason. Now is the time for you to become a published author.

If you're looking for additional help and inspiration as you begin the process of writing and publishing your first book, I would highly encourage you to check out my program at www.Self-PublishingPro.com

Just so you know the people that I enjoy working with are as follows:

- They are purpose driven
- They like accountability
- They enjoy motivational reminders
- They don't quit
- They like following step by step instructions

I am proud to say, every person who has joined as a member in Self-Publishing Pro has come out victorious as a best-selling author!

It'll be one of best investments you will ever make in yourself.

Like Warren Buffet once said "The best investment you can make is in yourself" because you are you own biggest asset by far."

My program will provide you with all the guidelines you need, and hold your hand through all the step-by-step instructions which were impossible to include in this book.

If publishing a book is something you want to accomplish then we really should connect. If you want to build a passive income, grow your current business, fulfill a passion project or become an authority on a topic, enrolling in Self-Publishing Pro can help you realize your goals – as it has for so many before you.

I've created a free, 4-video training session for those who are committed to writing and launching their own book. You can access this video training at http://self-publishingpro.com/freetraining. You will also find additional information about the Self-Publishing Pro Program there.

Regardless of whether you decide to enroll in this program, I would be forever grateful if you would share your success story with me.

Drop me a line when you publish your book, and let me know the ways in which it has transformed your life. Reach out to me at Justin@Self-PublishingPro.com.

Fortune favors the bold, so be bold my friends!

Justin Ledford

Acknowledgments

Writing a book is no small effort, so I would like to thank my amazing wife who has been a huge influence and partner to all my endeavors. She read this book and helped with the edits more than anyone, she is the best partner I could ever ask for and one of the smartest people I know.

I also want to give thanks to my team who always gives their best efforts to every project. To my friends who are also my mentors, I am always learning and striving because of your friendship. Mike Lonzetta for pushing me towards greatness when I was just getting started. And my family who always support my ventures and have given me a place to call home. Also, huge thanks for all the mentors and leaders in the personal growth community, you may not know me but I know you. Your contributions have made this world a better place. I am most thankful to The Creator who has given me the life & inspiration to follow my dreams.

Thank You for Reading My Book!

I sincerely appreciate all of your helpful feedback, and would love to hear what you have to say.

Your testimonials are what will help to make the next version even better.

Please leave me a supportive review by going to my Amazon book listing for **Book Launch Formula** and tell me what you think in a review

Always Grateful!!!

- Justin Ledford

Made in the USA
San Bernardino, CA
26 July 2017